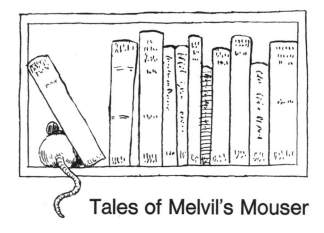

Tales of Melvil's Mouser

Tales

# of Melvil's Mouser

or *Much Ado About Libraries*

PAUL DUNKIN

R.R. BOWKER COMPANY
New York & London 1970

TO TOMMY

Published by R. R. Bowker Company (A Xerox Company),
1180 Avenue of the Americas, New York, N.Y. 10036

International Standard Book Number: 0-8352-0467-7
Library of Congress Catalog Card Number: 74-131911

Manufactured in the United States of America.

Illustrations by Bob Van Nutt

CONTENTS

Enter the Mouser

"The time was when a library was very like a museum, and a librarian was a mouser in musty books, and visitors looked with curious eyes at ancient tomes and manuscripts. The time *is* when a library is a school, and the librarian is in the highest sense a teacher, and the visitor is a reader among the books as a workman among his tools. Will any man deny to the high calling of such a librarianship the title of profession?"—Melvil Dewey in *Library Journal* Vol. 1, No. 1 (Sept. 30, 1876).

Thus Melvil Dewey thrust his mouser onto the stage of life almost 100 years ago. What ever happened to Melvil's mouser?

Some there are who scoff. They proclaim that the mouser dug in his heels; that he never came out of the stacks at all. Ominously they warn that the mouser had better get moving if he is not to be crushed by the information explosion and the computer. Or they shout that he must wake up to the ghetto and take to the streets—or that he must wake up to Vietnam and take to the streets.

Others insist that—whatever the mouser did or does—he does not follow a profession at all. Still others hold with Melvil that the mouser does so have a profession.

Everybody who is somebody and often somebody who is not has written a book or at least an article on the philosophy and profession of librarianship. They have clad the mouser in ermine; they have had the mouser roar—or they have sneered that the mouser's new clothes are like the emperor's new clothes.

The essays which follow have no such lofty aims. They seek only to tell of some of the mouser's adventures in the world of today—the world into which Father Melvil pushed him so unceremoniously 100 years ago. They do not pretend to be the truth, the whole truth, and nothing but. Indeed, what adventure is ever pure truth? Only the touch of fancy makes an adventure truly an adventure.

A Committee for all Who Mourn

"Censorship!" The Library Board Chairman put on his open face and it smiled a winning smile. Automatically the Committee Investigator smiled back.

The Chairman continued: "Censorship? Why, of course not. At no time did we ever think of that. Oh, we had a bit of rough going now and then. Like when he insisted that the Library have *Neverblue* on the open shelves where young people and even school kids could get at it. Imagine! It says right on the cover it is only for mature adults. I subscribe to *Neverblue* myself and I know. *My* kids never get to see it, that's for sure. But *Neverblue* was no reason for letting him go. After all we had hired him to run the Library and even if we did have to stop him on this *Neverblue* thing we had a lot of respect for him because he stood right up to us about it."

The open face winning smile turned into an open face earnest frown.

"Then why did you let him go?" The Investigator answered earnest frown with curious frown.

"Well, you see it was this way." The Chairman picked his words with care. "He's a nice young feller, but he was always stirring things up. Like—you know. Well—like the Bible Controversy."

"Bible Controversy?" The Investigator's frown deepened. "What was the Bible Controversy?"

"Oh, I'm sure he never mentioned it in his complaint to you people," smiled the Chairman. "That's just like him. He would not, I am sure, mention anything that had no bearing on the case." The Chairman smiled generously.

"But what was the Bible Controversy?" The Investigator was not a man to be put off easily; the Chairman of the National Library Association Intellectual Freedom Group had made him Investigator for just that reason.

"Well, you know how it is. Like every small town we have a professional trouble maker." The Chairman grinned apologetically. "Young Mrs. Blackstone is ours. She turned sour after Johnny Blackstone was killed in Vietnam. We gave Johnny a first class funeral—didn't cost her a cent either—and we made the day a town holiday and we even named the Library for him. But Hettie turned sour anyway. Nothing was ever right anywhere; you know."

The Investigator clucked.

"Hettie joined a Civil Rights Group and she marched in the streets; and she joined a Peacenix Group and she sat in at City Hall. Then she brought suit about the Bible being read in school. Said something about if there were a God Johnny would never have had to die in Vietnam and the school had no right to force the Bible on young Johnny. You can sort of understand how she felt but—you know."

The Investigator clucked again.

"Well, anyway, then he got into the act. Clippings about the suit stuck up in the Library; posters about Church and School; a display of books for and against atheism. You know the sort of thing I mean. Oh, nothing really serious. But it did make him a bit sore when we protested. We just had to tell him again that the Library is public property and the Librarian is a public servant. And everybody in town believes in the Bible; why Johnny taught a Sunday School class before he went to Vietnam."

It had been a long speech. The Chairman leaned back to rest in righteousness.

"I see." The Investigator's face was cold. Clearly he did not see. The Chairman rushed back into the fray.

"Then he began to be seen around town with Hettie Blackstone. Oh, everyone was sure it was on the up and up—no hankey-pankey—you know. But you know how it is in a small town. People will talk. And Hettie is a right pretty woman. They even said she was the reason why he got all mixed up in the Bible Controversy in the first place."

"Was that all?" The Investigator's face was blank.

"They say he even helped pay her lawyer—you know with money the town had paid him in salary. It was almost like spending public money to sue the town."

"Then the *Neverblue* case and the Bible Controversy were the reasons why you fired him?"

"No, like I told you, the *Neverblue* thing had nothing to do with it." The Chairman was patient and plaintive. "And we didn't fire him. We didn't fire him at all."

"Then what did you do?"

"We just did not renew his contract in January. But we didn't fire him; we let him finish out his contract. That was all we had ever agreed to do."

"Well, call it what you wish." The Investigator was growing weary. "The only reason why you did not renew his contract was the Bible Controversy?"

"Well, I suppose you could put it that way if you had a mind to." The Chairman's voice was pure oil. "Really, though, the problem was much bigger than the Bible Controversy. That was just a sample of the stuff he was pulling all the time. It got so no one in town trusted him any more —you know—"

"I see," said the Investigator for the second time. He closed his book and he tried to smile. "Thank you, Mr. Jujpar. You have been very helpful."

"So, you see," explained the Investigator to the full Committee. "It was not a tenure job and we have only his word against their word, and censorship was not involved at all."

"Did you talk to Mrs. Blackstone?" The earnest young man with the neat brown beard had welcomed assignment to this Committee. Now maybe he could help.

"Well, no, it seemed hardly worth while." The Investigator sighed; ah, to be young again! "She would, no doubt, simply have borne out the Chairman's story—with a different emphasis, of course. But that would not have changed the point at issue."

"Did you talk to anyone on the list of names he gave you?" It was a persistent young man.

"No, I did not." The Investigator sighed again. "They would all have said he is a good young man, a good librarian, and that he was good for the town. But that would be all subjective opinion; none of it would be hard fact. He simply managed to get into a small town scrap on the wrong side."

"I can't see how we can do anything at all about it." The Chairman of the Committee was grim and firm. "Maybe it was censorship or maybe it was only this Bible thing. But we can't prove it. What's more: If we get NLA involved in this mess, then every guy in the country who gets fired or even gets a beef will complain and we won't have time for anything except work on this Committee."

The young man shot his last arrow: "We could at least have invited him to join us for this meeting and tell his side."

The Chairman frowned. So did the Committee.

A Fact is a Fact—Or is it?

The Firethorn State Library Association was in annual meeting. There was the usual crop of solid sessions with solid papers on how we changed our charging system good and why we are switching from Dewey to LC good and other such solid matters. Alongside the usual solid sessions were the usual fluid clatches in bars, halls and coffee houses. Here there was little talk of charging and switching. There was much talk of the Clammer-Banger Affair.

Mrs. Artie Clammer of the Children's Department of the Firethorn Public Library was a writer of letters. The local newspapers, the state and national journals, the library journals—each carried its fair share of Mrs. Clammer's protests against this and that injustice inflicted by the establishment. Even in the *National Journal of Genealogy* Mrs. Clammer was not unknown to fame.

But that was before she met up with Mrs. Samson Banger.

It all began when the Students' Committee for Democracy Now printed in secret and sold in public a satire on sex which the Trustees of Firethorn State University had branded as pornographic. The cops grabbed the students, the newspapers grabbed the story, and Mrs. Clammer grabbed her pen.

Righteous indignation singed the Clammer paper: Censorship in the State University! Where was Justice? It was one of Mrs. Clammer's better productions, and she flipped it proudly onto the desk of her boss, Bableton Braggs. But Mr. Braggs was in the throes of writing a budget which would please both his staff and his Library Board. He had no time to wade through another Clammer letter; no doubt, it was all the same old harmless line. Censorship, freedom, all that stuff that everybody talked about and then forgot about. Braggs grinned absently at Mrs. Clammer and murmured "Excellent! OK!" or words to that effect. Then he bent back over his budget.

The newspaper editor grinned broadly at Mrs. Clammer and he shouted "Excellent! OK!" or words to that effect. He slapped Mrs. Clammer's letter onto the front page with headline: "Public Library Official Says State University Censorship is Obscene." And he wrote a solemn editorial to berate the University for censorship and congratulate the Public Library for chastizing its sister institution. It was Mrs. Clammer's finest hour.

Firethorn buzzed. Firethorn State University buzzed. The whole state buzzed. Library journals, big and little, buzzed.

Enter Mrs. Samson Banger. She burned.

Mrs. Samson Banger presided over the Firethorn Public Library Board. The Board met—long and loud and earnest. Who were these students anyway? Black-bearded, long haired, radical left wingers, no doubt. Who was Mrs. Clammer anyway? Another radical left-winger, no doubt. Why did she think she could speak for the Public Library? And where was Bableton Braggs while his staff was writing all this rot about sex instead of shelving books? Mr. Braggs dragged out his excuse: He had been so busy working at the budget . . . Mrs. Banger shouted that the Library would be lucky to get any budget now.

Mrs. Banger was a true prophet. The City Council hated pornography; it hated squabbling; it hated appropriations;

most of all it hated publicity—bad publicity, that is. The City Council had had its publicity bad and Mr. Braggs had his budget slashed.

The Public Library Board reprimanded Bableton Braggs; the Board reprimanded Mrs. Clammer. Mrs. Banger wrote the reprimands. The Braggs reprimand froze; the Clammer reprimand sizzled. Mrs. Clammer resigned. The Library Board rejected Mrs. Clammer's resignation; then the Board fired her.

The story made all the newspapers—local, state, even national. It got into the library journals. Editorials inquired why the National Library Association did nothing. The National Library Association turned the matter over to its Committee on Freedom.

And now the Firethorn State Library Association was in annual meeting. Everybody talked of the Clammer-Banger Affair. The Firethorn State Library Association had no Committee on Freedom. A Committee of Twenty appointed itself. The Committee of Twenty would deal with the Clammer-Banger Affair.

The annual business meeting of the Firethorn State Library Association had always been dull. This year it was not. The Committee of Twenty broke into the placid agenda to present a Statement. It was short and snappy. "We are not interested in placing blame in the Clammer-Banger Affair. We want only the facts. Not just censorship is at stake here. Even more important is the relation of a librarian—any librarian—to his board."

Mrs. Samson Banger asked the Chair to allow a response from Dr. Simeon Satyr, revered Director of the Firethorn State University Library and also a member of the Firethorn Public Library Board.

Dr. Satyr rambled through the history of the case. Actually censorship in libraries was not at stake at all. Mrs. Clammer had simply used Public Library stationery to protest what she thought was University censorship of pornography. The University was not involved, however, because the young men had been arrested by the Firethorn town police on town property. It had been damaging to the Public Library to allow one of its staff to attack another publicly supported institution, and the Public Library Board had done only what was proper: Censure the Director of the Public Library and censure Mrs. Clammer. Mrs. Clammer had not been content with this; she had resigned. She had not been content with resigning; she had phoned Mrs. Banger. Mrs. Banger did not even know Mrs. Clammer and she had not wanted to talk with her. Mrs. Banger had said nothing. But then Mrs. Banger had been harangued with foul and filthy language. So the Board had voted not to accept Mrs. Clammer's resignation, but to terminate her services. And that was all the story, ladies and gentlemen. Newspapers and the library press had made a big thing out of half truths and lies offered by protagonists of Mrs. Clammer.

Dr. Satyr received a standing ovation.

Jack Demy, young and bearded, then rose and made a statement. Jack was Chairman of the National Library Association Committee on Freedom, and he had come there only to find out the facts. The NLA had no wish for a witch hunt. Obviously the liberal press and liberal librarians everywhere had fallen down in this case. There would be other situations, and someone would have to stand up and ask for the facts. This had not been done in the Clammer-Banger Affair; it would be done next time. On behalf of the National Library Association Committee on Freedom he presented an apology to Dr. Satyr and Mrs. Banger.

There was a smattering of applause. The Chairman raised his gavel to close the meeting.

Hi Firum, also young, also bearded, jumped to his feet.

Hi was Chairman of the Committee of Twenty, and he was angry.

"What *are* the facts, sir? Dr. Satyr says that Mrs. Banger says that Mrs. Clammer said that she was resigning and that Mrs. Banger says that Mrs. Clammer said it with foul and filthy language. We have not heard from Mrs. Banger and we have not heard from Mrs. Clammer. We have not heard the words which Dr. Satyr says Mrs. Banger says were foul and filthy. Would we all agree that they were foul and filthy? The National Library Association should not pull out so eagerly. Of course, we want the facts. But what *are* . . ."

The gavel banged the meeting to a close. It was long past time for the annual banquet and in the next room ice for the cocktails was melting.

A Fool and His Money

Quiggsby's wife writes all the checks. That is ok with Quiggsby. Quiggsby hates arithmetic. But now and then there is a snag.

"Lancelot," said Mrs. Quiggsby, "why is the National Library Association check this year $50.00? It was only $40.00 last year."

Quiggsby looked up from his novel. "Well, I guess it's because of my raise last year."

"Your raise, Lancelot, was only $500—remember?" Lancelot did, indeed, remember. It had pleased him just to get a raise; it had pleased his wife not at all because it was so late and so little. She went on: "A five percent increase for you means a 50 percent increase for NLA. You're lucky the library was so stingy; a ten per cent increase for you and the NLA would have grabbed it all. What do you get for all that money, anyway?"

Quiggsby sighed and laid down the novel. Too bad; just at the most exciting part, too.

"Well, I'm a member, and they say it takes over $15.00 just to keep a membership going—you know, the records and all that stuff. They say there are over 30,000 members." Quiggsby was strangely proud of that 30,000.

"How come it takes so much? What do they do besides write down whether you've paid or not? Haven't they heard about computers? Well, anyway, even if they are so old fashioned it takes $15.00 just to keep track of your payment that leaves a profit of $35.00. What do you get for $35.00?"

"Well—I get the NLA *Bulletin* because I'm a member and I belong to two divisions because I'm a member and I get the publications of the divisions—"

"You mean that stack of old magazines in the attic? I was about to throw them out last spring; *I* didn't know they were so valuable. *You* never read them. Why don't you read them if they cost you $35.00?"

Quiggsby cast a longing look at the novel. "Well, I'm so tired when I come home at night. It takes a lot out of a guy being on his feet all day and answering stupid questions with a smile. I want TV or a good book; I don't want more stuff about a library."

"I know, dear."

Her smile was so sweetly patient Quiggsby rushed on defensively: "Anyway, they are full of stuff about how to run a big library or how much it costs to catalog a book or how some big shot has moved on to a bigger job or some big project in some fancy library. They're just not about my kind of job and my kind of library. Oh, now and then they do have something about my kind of job but usually it is by some library boss or library school professor who has a lot of crazy theories about how I should do it even if he's never done it himself."

Mrs. Q. was indignant. "You mean they charge you $35.00 just for magazines like that?"

"Well, I reckon it does take money to run a convention every year. They say there were 6500 people and over 800 meetings in Kansas City last year."

"Maybe so, but *you* didn't go. Mr. Quinsy said there weren't any travel funds, remember? And they usually hold those conventions in San Francisco or Chicago or somewhere else at the end of the earth. I think it's unfair to make you help pay for a convention you can't go to."

"Well, really, I guess maybe they don't. They charge a
registration fee for people who do go, you know. They even
charge a fee for Midwinter when there aren't any program
meetings."

Quiggsby smiled apologetically and hopefully and started
to reach for the novel. But Quiggsby's wife was not to be
put off.

"If your $35.00 doesn't go for conventions you don't at-
tend, then where *does* it go?" A sudden thought sent her
on a new quest: "I'm sure glad it doesn't go for conventions
because you said there are 30,000 members and only 6500
were in Kansas City. Think how unfair it would be if 24,000
people had to help pay for 6500 other people in a convention. But 30,000 times $35.00 would be a lot of money.
Where *does* it all go?"

Quiggsby had an inspiration. "Well, you see, there's a big
Headquarters Office in Chicago and every division has an
executive secretary and there's an Executive Director for
the whole business and—"

"What on earth do all those people *do*, Lancelot?"

Quiggsby sighed. That shot had backfired for sure. "Oh,
they do things to make it easier for the elected officers and
they get a lot of mail and send a lot of mail—"

"Mail about what, Lancelot?"

"Oh, I reckon mail about NLA programs and mail about
articles in the publications and—"

"You mean, they spend all that money just to have programs that only a fifth of the members attend and just to
have magazines that the members don't read?"

"Well, they have some kind of an international relations
office; I suppose that takes *some* money."

"But, Lancelot, I thought the President and the Secretary of State take care of international relations. We pay
taxes for that; why should NLA put its oar in?"

"Well, there's National Library Week; that takes a lot of planning."

"You mean that crazy thing they have every year about 'Be all You Can Be: Read' or some other silly slogan when you all have to spend extra time on committees and things planning all sorts of weird publicity stunts? If they pay money for *that* they should pay some to *you*—not charge you for it."

"Well, NLA does have one of the best lobbys in Washington, they say."

"What does it *do*, Lancelot? Does it lobby for a national minimum wage for librarians? Does it lobby for money to keep the library going next year if the City Council does cut the library out of the budget? We could sure use some federal money in this town's library."

Quiggsby dropped back into his last ditch defense. "Well, a professional man should support his professional organization."

"Why, Lancelot?"

But Quiggsby did not reply. He was worn out. Mrs. Q. was worn out too.

So she wrote the check.

A Job for all Seasons

Callimachus bowed low before Ptolemy. "Sire, may you live forever."

The young man shuddered: "What a dreadful prospect!" Then he smiled gaily. "But what do you really want to tell me, Cal?"

The old man's voice was deep and slow. "Sire, I have the honor to report that the task assigned me by your honored father so long ago is at last completed. Now let me go to my reward. While life remains I want to write the epic."

Ptolly really liked the solemn old man, but he couldn't for the life of him remember what this great task had been. He stalled. "The reward you may have, of course; you have earned it. But first tell me something of how you went about the task."

Cal warmed. A good young man in spite of all the stories . . . "Our literature was in a shambles. Every text was in many different copies. No one knew what had been written and what had not and no one knew what text was correct. Your never-to-be-forgotten father—"

"So what did you do about it, Cal?" Ptolly was not noted for his patience.

"Sire, for each text we looked at all the manuscripts and then we prepared a correct version. All the manuscripts are now organized in one logical whole and all are now recorded. Each can now be found at once, no matter how you refer to it. Never again will anyone do an experiment that has already been done, argue a point that has already been argued out, write a book that someone else has already written. Everything that anyone has ever thought and written is preserved for all time and everything can be found for all time."

Ptolly whistled. "Splendid, Cal, splendid!" Then his Puckish grin: "But how do you know it was all worth preserving?"

Cal allowed himself a smile; the young man was on the ball for sure. He bowed. "That, Sire, is what I suggested to your honored father long ago when he asked me to undertake the task. His reply was that only the readers could judge that."

Ptolly was taken aback. Wise old guy, his father, after all. He rather wished he had managed to see more of him. But only for a moment; then he thought of something else: "But that's only for the books written up till now. What of the books now being written? What will you do with them, my learned and thoughtful Keeper of the King's Library?"

Cal smiled in forced modesty. "Sire, in the presence of carrying out the task we discovered a new science: Information Science, we call it and it is the science of knowing all about information and its mysterious ways. We have mastered this science. We have made the record of books past, we shall simply add to the record books present and books future. There is more, Sire. Even now your royal mathematicians and your royal craftsmen are building a machine which will do much of the work for us."

Ptolly was filled with wonder. "But, Cal, where will this all end? Already you have asked us to build two new library buildings since the task began and they are now filled to overflowing and you and your staff are in a third and now this machine . . . Cal, where *will* it end?"

Cal lapsed into shocked silence. Had the Grand Dream

become master of him, Callimachus, learned information scientist and poet?

Ptolly's dazed words struggled on: "As our great civilization spreads, more and more backward nations will learn our ways and more and more people will learn to write and once they learn they will write and write. More and more information will pour into your information science machine and what goshawful stuff some of it will be! The land will be jammed with buildings for your information science records and buildings for those infernal machines."

Ptolly broke off into wild laughter: "Worst of all, Cal, there will be millions of *your* people! Remember what Timon of Phlius said about you?

> Egypt has its mad recluses,
> Book bewildered anchorites,
> In the hen-coop of the Muses
> Keeping up their endless fights.

Golly! What a crew! And there'll have to be buildings—excuse me, Cal, hen-coops—for them too. Librarians!"

Cal gulped. Timon of Phlius indeed! Timmy had been only jealous! He'd have been glad to come running into the hen-coop if he'd been asked.

"It seemed like a good idea once, Sire." Cal felt he had to say something; once it was said it sounded lame indeed.

"That's all right, Cal." Ptolly was really sorry for the downcast old man. "It'll all work out somehow."

"But now that it's started, Sire, it will last forever."

"That's it, Cal! You've hit on the answer. Will it last forever? Can anything last forever?"

Cal was not noted for originality in his poems; his master's philosophy left him as cold as his master's sense of humor.

Ptolly went on slowly: "Euripides, Aristophanes, Plato—they were there before we came along and before you dug up your Information Science. We don't have any like them today. Is Information Science with its talk of preserving everything and organizing everything—is it the beginning of something or the end of something? Suppose we are the end of something. Is there any hope for the return of Euripides and Plato and originality and all the rest until we and our organized library go the way of all flesh?"

Suddenly he brightened. "Who knows, Cal? Maybe we *shall* be destroyed."

Cal's shocked face sobered Ptolly just as he remembered the dancing girl waiting in the next room.

"Cheer up, Cal. I have my moods. Forgive me. We can work it out somehow. No doubt you are right. No doubt your system will last forever. This mighty kingdom and this mighty library. How can we fail?"

Anybody Got Fifteen Cents?

On April 1 dawn came just as it had on every other day to the big ugly city nestled by the big ugly swamp. Four hundred thousand men and women and children got out of bed one way or another, shaved, showered, gulped their Wheaties, brushed their teeth, and hustled off to school and work and shopping centers exactly as they had on every other day. Outside Megapol in the suburbs four hundred thousand other people jammed the street cars and buses and automobiles and poured into the city exactly as they had on every other day.

Except that no one came to the Library. This was the day the Library was to close. Back in mid-February the Megapol City Council had decided that this was the only way they could cut the bankrupt city's tax rate by fifteen cents.

Could the Library really close? The President did not think so. He even issued a Proclamation: Libraries, he said, are arsenals of the accumulated knowledge and wisdom of mankind; indeed, by expanding the horizons of even one American, our libraries serve us all. Megapol Public Library had long been in the forefront in this creative role. He closed with a ringing statement: He wanted to make one thing crystal clear: He was confident that the state and local governments and especially the private sector of the economy would get Megapol through this crisis, and he looked forward to Megapol Library's continuing achievements in the challenging decades that lie ahead.

The Governor issued a Proclamation: The State was overwhelmed by this impending tragedy. Megapol Public Library had long served not simply Megapol but the entire northern half of the State. Megapol Library had indeed been officially designated as the Metropolitan Reference Library for that half of the state. Megapol Library should have financial help from the State, but the Legislature (of the same political faith as the President) had refused to help. The Governor's appeals to the federal government for help had gone unanswered. But the Governor was convinced that the local government would surely be able to find some money somewhere; he did not understand what the President had in mind when he talked of the "private sector of the economy" because Megapol was a public library.

The President of the National Library Association issued a Proclamation: Megapol Public Library had had a long and distinguished career; it was famous both at home and abroad. It was unthinkable that this career should end for fifteen cents. He was instructing the NLA lobby in Washington to go to work at once on the members of Congress. There ought to be a special appropriation to help get Megapol through this crisis. He was sure the money could be found and he looked forward to a long and distinguished future for the Megapol Public Library.

The President of the State Library Association issued a Proclamation: Megapol Public Library had served its community and the entire state long and well. Surely a grateful State would not let such long and faithful service stop so suddenly just because of what seemed to be a lack of funds. He asked the SLA Legislative Committee to get to work at once on members of the Legislature, and he urged every member of the SLA to write his Assemblyman. Surely the

Legislature could find the money somewhere and surely Megapol Public Library would continue its faithful service to the State.

The Dean of the Library School in Megapol's state issued a statement to the press: For many years the Library School's research had been proving that libraries in big cities were in big trouble, but no one had paid much attention. Now the dangerous neglect of the School's research had led to massive tragedy. An old and distinguished library in a large city could actually be closed because of lack of funds. This was a serious development; other cities would begin to think they could save fifteen cents this way too. The Library School was making application at once for a huge government grant to finance a study of precisely what factors were involved in such a colossal tragedy. Once the causes were identified, another study might be able to show how such disasters could be avoided in the future.

Over the country famous authors wrote famous articles about how much the library had meant to them when they had been starving sons and daughters of starving parents. In spite of their lowly state they had always been welcome to the library where the magic touch of books and their magic content and the magic atmosphere of the library had made them the civilized creators they were today. Over the country school and college leaders, Congressmen, newspapers, labor leaders, and business men sang the praises of libraries and damned the shortsighted plan of Megapol to save fifteen cents on its Library.

In middle March the City Council held a public meeting to consider the Library and the budget. Some four hundred people attended.

The Director of Megapol Public Library, a nationally famous librarian, arose and made a statement: For over three hundred years Megapol had had some kind of library; and some of the country's best known librarians had governed it. Last year the Library had served over a million readers. There were school libraries, branches, sub-branches, hospital units, a business library—a massive service to Megapol and the whole state. He had heard hints that the threat to close the Library was a ploy to call attention to Megapol's financial crisis and get State and Federal aid. He hoped that this was not true; the Library should not be made a pawn in political financial games.

It was a stormy meeting. After four hours the Mayor's gavel brought it to a close and the Mayor made a statement:

"Last year the Library served over a million readers. But the town which owns that library has only 400,000 people. More than half are black and many live at a poverty or below-poverty level. Sixty percent of Megapol's land is untaxable. Four hundred thousand people—and only 400 of them here tonight! Why? Because they need something more than books. This city has some things it must do or it will simply fall apart. Fire, police, hospitals, schools; the budget takes care of these things—not as much as it should but as much as it can. The only other items in the budget is our anti-poverty program. Food, clothing, housing, job training; from which of these shall we take fifteen cents for the Library? These 400,000 are my people. I do not intend to neglect the basic needs of my people just so some guy fifty miles away can find out about Alaska's fishing. The Library building is sound; the books are all there. Both will keep till we have enough money to open them again."

On April 1 dusk came just as it had on every other day to the big ugly city nestled by the big ugly swamp. Four hundred thousand people hustled off home exactly as they had on every other day. Four hundred thousand other people jammed the street cars and buses and automobiles and poured out of the city just as they had on every other day.

Except that no one came out of the Library.

Are You Relevant, Buster?

Relevance once meant something (no one person ever knew exactly what) in the mystic world of information science. Now the word has swept on to bigger and (no doubt) better things. Is the library relevant to the world of today? Is the library school relevant? Is the librarian relevant? Are *you* relevant, Buster?

Then get with it, man. Live in the today world. Do you know that 65.7 per cent of Bluestone University's faculty does not feel that the Bluestone University libraries are one of the three most attractive or three least attractive features of the Bluestone environment? The library is just one of those so-so things; who knows or cares about it? What is good enough for Bluestone is good enough for the world, isn't it?

What happened to all the cash Uncle Sam was handing out to libraries? Like a drop of water in hell, that's what. Not that it was such a big drop to begin with. Two bits per U.S. citizen for books and over 21 thousand bucks for lead to be put in *each* North Vietnamese and Viet Cong in South Vietnam. Now the two bits are there no longer. To Uncle Sam the library is just one of those so-so things; who knows or cares about it? What is good enough for Uncle Sam is good enough for the world, isn't it?

What happened when the riots blazed in the big cities? Where was the library then? Handing out fire and bread to the rioters? Do libraries mean no more to the poor than they mean to the Bluestone men? Just one of those so-so things; who knows or cares about it? What is good enough for the poor is good enough for the world, isn't it?

What happened when the information explosion burst on an unsuspecting world? What was the library doing then? Counting overdue books and collecting fines, that's what. And the interloping documentalists and information scientists wheeled in their jargon and their machine. To the seeker for information the library is just one of those so-so things; who knows or cares about it? What is good enough for the information seeker is good enough for the world, isn't it?

So get with it, Buster; join the now world. Be relevant. If you are not relevant the library will go the way of the dinosaur. And you will lose your cushy job with its big salary and its groovy fringe benefits. You may even have to join the disadvantaged. You wouldn't like that, would you?

Be relevant. Make the library relevant. Be a dynamic social force in the whole world.

Be relevant. Find out what the Bluestone University prof wants before he knows it himself. (The Library School Ph.D. students will tell you what it is if you can't find out.) Have it on the prof's desk Monday morning. Then he'll have some idea about whether he likes you or not. Everybody likes a relevant man and a relevant woman. The prof will even pound the President's desk and ask for you to get academic status. You'd like that, wouldn't you?

Be relevant. Get on the picket line against the Vietnam war. Burn your draft card and bring a match to the other guys in line. Wave a Viet Cong flag. Shout and grow a beard. Stop the war and bring all that ammunition back and get your money back—every cent of the 21 thousand bucks they say it takes to shoot each Vietnamese and Viet Cong. Maybe you can get the twenty five cents for every man's book raised to fifty cents. They'll have to spend that 21 thousand somehow; why not on a library and a librarian in the now world? You'd like that, wouldn't you?

Be relevant. When the picket line stops at night, join the riots in the city streets. Burn, baby, burn! Get bread for the hungry. Get a roof for the homeless. Get clothing for the cold. Get medicine for the sick. How do you get them? Just reach through the window and take them, Buster. Remember relevant riot course 658 back in good old relevant library school? All the world loves a rioter especially when he's relevant. You want to be loved, don't you?

Be relevant. Jump headfirst into that information explosion. Get with the future, Buster! Get those consoles off the drawing board and into the assembly line. Get a console into every home. Get two; get three; but get them. Even in the ghetto let every man, every woman, every child do his own thing with his console. And you won't either be a dinosaur. And you won't either have to lose your cushy job with its groovy fringe benefits. And you won't either have to join the disadvantaged; you took care of them anyway in the riots—remember?

So be relevant, Buster. But do it right away. Remember what information science did with relevance. Tomorrow relevance may not be the in-word with library science either.

Back to the Mountain

Every dog has its day and who is to say that a batch of old laws is better than a dog?

Long ago the Wise Man of the East lugged down from Mt. Biblon the new laws for us. Like the First Wise Man toting down the first laws, he found us eating and drinking and making merry with the golden calf of tradition. The First Wise Man blew his top and smashed the tablets of the first laws; and he had to trudge back up the mountain for new copies. Not so our new sage. Our new sage kept his cool and his tablets and sat down and wrote a book. Then he wrote another book. And then he wrote another. And then, and then, and then, and then. He wrote a whole library about the new laws. And on the back side of every title page—lo, the new laws in all their majesty. He who runs may read; even he who rapid-reads cannot escape them.

Not all new things are different from the old; these new laws are. There are not two tablets of them; they fill only one. There are not ten laws; there are only five. This is the jet age, friend. Get with it. No time to waste on more laws than you need. They are not negative—thou shalt not and all that jazz. They are today-laws, they accent the positive. They are not fleshly—who will covet his neighbor's wife or kill a cop when he can have a library book around? These laws are spiritual; they tell it like it is, one eternal truth after another.

Take the first one; Books are for use. There it is, only four little words. Magnificent. Books are the constant companions of man. From De Bury and before to Larry Powell and after, we have heard it again and again always in many words. Now we have it in a few. Books are for use. True. Books adorn our minds and our living rooms. In our hands they teach us, and on our shelves they brag to others of how bright they have made us even if we have not read them. They prop doors open and they elevate children from adults' chairs to the dining table. They store roses and photos, pencils and cash. They keep us warm if we burn them and they lull us to sleep if we read them. After we have read them we can use them for other things—even an old Sears Roebuck catalog had its use until we fell from grace and gave up the codex for the roll again. Books lay open their pages to the child's crayon and his grandfather's specs. Books can be hurled at saint and sinner; and great is the crash thereof. No doubt about it: Books are for use.

Now look at Number 2: Every reader his book. Here again is Great Truth. In this best of all possible worlds, why should not every reader have his book? If he cannot buy it, he can go to his friendly little library. Better yet, let the book come to him—in the Good Humor truck along with the chocolate covered ice cream cone. Let him feed his brain while he feeds his face. No truth like an old truth: Explore inner space; read. Every reader his book. The book may be jammed with four letter words or the sayings of Chairman Mao. So what? It is his book, is it not and he is a reader, is he not? Every reader his book, friend, and that's an end to *that*. Even so, this Great Truth, like many another great truth, has a murky side. What of the non-reader? Is he to have his non-book? Sure he is. It may be a marble or a globe, a map or a microfilm, a jazz band or a poet reading aloud. Every non-reader his non-book, friend, and make no mistake about it. Else libraries will fade away like old generals. What would you do for a living *then?* No doubt the Sage from the East meant to say also a deeper saying: "By book I mean also non-book." But even *that* deep saying leaves the Sage on the hook. What if the reader wants no book at all after all? What if he wants only a page from a book? Or only a sentence from a page? Or only an idea from a sentence? Tear it out and let him have it, of course. Better yet, stick a console in his cottage. Verily the Master, like Homer, nodded on this one. Had he been awake, the Sage would have said it like it is: Every consoler his console.

The Third Law moves in deeper mystery: Every book its reader. Did the Great Man nod again here? Did he mean: Every non-book its non-reader? No doubt. After all he did mean to say: "By book I mean non-book." And yet, is a marble or a globe, a map or a microfilm, a jazz band or a poet reading aloud—are these and all other non-books only for non-readers? Are we fair to non-books if we hem them in so? Of course, we agreed also that the Sage really must have meant consoles anyway. Every console its consoler; that way it makes sense. Only one more sticker: Does, indeed, every book or every non-book or every page or every idea *deserve* a reader? Were it not better for most of them and for most of us if they were cast into the outer darkness? In the day of twenty-four hours have we time even for all of the best? Without birth control for books and non-books, pages and ideas, how can we hope to follow the Third Law even from afar? But whose book will be birth controlled? Not the one I write surely, probably not even the book you write, dear reader. But whose?

We are in luck with the Fourth Law; it drops books. Save the time of the reader. But how can we save the time of the reader if we shove a book or a non-book or a console under his nose every time he stops to breathe? Where will he find the time he is to save? Will he even *want* to save time if he can use that time only to read another book or non-read another non-book or peek into that console again? Eating, drinking, sleeping, playing, making love, making war—surely there is much to be done with time. No doubt the Master meant: Save the time of the reader, the non-reader, and the consoler from non-reading, non-non-reading and non-consoling respectively. But that comes to an awfully long law; he might need two tablets for the set after all. There is a Corollary which the Master sometimes sticks in after the Fourth Law: Save the time of the staff. After all they do need some time in the staff room for this and that. But how save the time of the staff? Send the readers and all the others home?

At last comes the Fifth Law: A library is a growing organism. So is a boy, so is a city, so is a cancer. So what? The boy needs new clothes, the city needs new houses, the cancer needs a knife. Growth brings change, but is change always or even generally good? We must, no doubt, adapt to change. But how? By giving it room or by cutting it out?

And there, dear reader, are the Five Laws of Library Science. Five Laws to take the place of Ten. Five Laws to change the world.

Trundle up the mountain once again, my Master.

Big Brother Has Four Hands

Young Brittlebright bustled into his Assistant's office and slapped the pamphlet onto her desk.

"Read it, Miss Micklehoffen, read it! Great little old book that. Young thinking. Big thinking. Just what we all need. Read it soon as you can."

Miss Micklehoffen glanced at the little book. "Oh, the Report of the National Advisory Committee on Libraries. I've read it already. Big thinking maybe—but not young thinking. Goodman Day's introduction could have come straight out of Richard De Bury or Larry Powell. Books are good for you. So what else is new? And the Committee's own introduction with all its talk of 'strong social benefit awareness'—talk fresh out of the 1930's and the New Deal."

Brittlebright was shocked. The generation gap was broad and deep. Richard De Bury and the Depression indeed! Good thing the Library had a rigid retirement plan! He came to with a bang: "At least, you will have to admit that the Report itself thinks big. Look at the title: *Library Services for the Nation's Needs: Toward Fulfillment of a National Policy.*

Miss Micklehoffen's voice was gentle and firm: "Maybe it's too big."

"*Too* big! What can you mean?" Brittlebright gulped. He grabbed the little book and began to read from the page:

"Today some Americans share the use of collections of millions of volumes, while others lack access even to meager and deficient library facilities." He flipped the page: "Some 20 million Americans, largely in rural areas, have no public library service at all, and some 10 million more have access only to very small libraries with very inadequate collections and little or no service from professional librarians." Brittlebright slapped the book back onto her desk in triumph. "What do you make of that? Still too big?"

"How many of all those millions of people, both those with access to libraries and those without it, actually need to read or even want to read? For that matter, how many *can* read? How many need bread more than books? The Committee should think of all these things if it really means that talk about 'strong social benefit awareness.' "

Brittlebright bristled. He grabbed the book again and read from the page: "More than two-thirds of all public libraries fail to meet National Library Association standards as to minimum adequate size of collections, and not one in 30 meets NLA standards for per capital support."

He dropped the book back onto the desk and allowed himself a triumphant smile.

Miss Micklehoffen was unimpressed. "But, Mr. Brittlebright, suppose every library in the country had as many books as the NLA standards say it should have and suppose every library in the country could find as much cash per head to lay out as the NLA standards say it should have. Would all those poor deprived millions come flocking into the libraries? Our library has all the books and dollars NLA says we should have, but where are all the people?" She swept her hand toward the window looking out on an empty reading room.

Brittlebright changed the subject. "You'll have to admit the Recommendations of the Committee are good."

"Just what *are* the Recommendations?"

"Why, they're spelled out in black and white!" Brittle-bright was a bit impatient. "First of all, there is to be a National Commission on Libraries and Information Science as a continuing federal planning agency."

Miss Micklehoffen yawned. "Big Brother of all the libraries and all the librarians! Big Brother will make plans to take care of all those millions of deprived people. Maybe not a chicken in every pot but a book on every table. And what will Big Brother do with all the plans when he has made them? Who will carry them out?"

"I don't know about your Big Brother business." Brittle-bright frowned. "But the Commission will be 'empowered to recommend legislation'; it says so right here."

Miss Mickelhoffen smiled meekly: "Do you know anyone who is not empowered to recommend legislation?"

Brittlebright's mouth fell open: "Well—just by existing and speaking out the Commission could do some good—you know, sort of like the United Nations and world peace."

Miss Micklehoffen smiled sweetly: "Yes, I suppose so. What else does the report recommend?"

"The second recommendation is for the Library of Congress."

"Big Brother's first hand," murmured Miss Micklehoffen. Her voice turned acid. "And what does the report do for LC? It simply tells it to go on doing what it has been doing and asks that LC be recognized as the national library and asks for a board of advisers to LC. Would this board change LC policy? Who knows? Probably not. LC has always gone its own way—remember how it squashed the cataloging-in-source idea when everybody else wanted it?"

Brittlebright was growing desperate: "What about the next Recommendation: To establish a Federal Institute of Library and Information Science?"

Miss Mickelhoffen smiled this time like Mona Lisa. "Big Brother's second hand? The Institute (so the Report says) will be the principal center for basic and applied research in all relevant areas. What is 'principal' and what is 'relevant'? Every agency mentioned in a Recommendation has responsibility for research of some sort. I suppose the Institute will specialize in computer and network research. The fashionable nod toward automation."

Brittlebright sighed. "I suppose you will say that the next Recommendation simply gives its blessing to more of the same from the Office of Education."

Miss Micklehoffen smiled brightly: "Big Brother's third hand. Yes, that's about it: more and better of what we have now. And the final Recommendation that state library agencies should be strengthened is a sound, pious wish for Big Brother's fourth hand."

Brittlebright sank into a chair.

Miss Mickelhoffen was not yet finished. "You know, I think four hands may be too many. Each hand may or may not know what the others are doing. Each hand may make a fist or clasp another hand in friendship. But don't forget Big Brother's feet. The Report says that it 'should be declared national policy, enunciated by the President and enacted into law by the Congress.' So the Report depends on a new President and a new Congress and the cash they will dig up. Big Brother has four hands and feet of clay."

Brittlebright marched into his office and closed the door and got out the organization chart of the Library.

Books Please

"Books please." The gay mobile flaunts itself just outside Professor Poofen's office door. Because Poofy is tall and skinny, he could bump his head against it as he passes. Perhaps that is why they hung it above a chair in the hall where sit students waiting to enroll in the snap courses (students, alas, think they can find them even in the good schools)—or to explain that through no fault of their own they missed the last question on that last exam.

"Books please." The pedant in Poofy comes awake. What do the words mean? Why, they can mean one of at least two different things.

1) "Books please." Just like that. A simple declarative statement, Mr. Pedant. And what do you make of that, Sir?

Well—do they now? *Do* books please? Depends on who and where you are, I reckon. Poofy sees few of them pleasing at a cocktail party or when you put up the storm windows or when you gossip with your neighbor or when you play bridge or golf.

Books do not please the housewife with a leaky faucet—unless one of them is a practical encyclopedia which sets forth in detail the mystery of leaky faucets and how to unleak them. And then it is a book, not books. Poofy's Pedant smiles.

Depends on other things too. Books do not please if they

are ugly or if you are moving and have to pack them or if you do not like what is in them. Can you say of *Mein Kampf*: It pleases? How about *The Politician*? And even if you do like what is in them, there are problems. If you are a Pogo fan the book does, of course, please. But even more the Pogo strip in the daily newspaper pleases.

There are, it seems after a short unscientific sampling of some of the factors of this problem, at least some times when books do not please at all—when, in fact, books are a darned nuisance. So "Books please" is no statement of universal truth.

Even if it were a statement of universal truth Poofy's poor little mobile says nothing new. From *Philobiblon* and before to *Books in My Baggage* and after, the message—such as it is—has been proclaimed from the rooftops.

There is still the second meaning, Mr. Fussy Pedant.

2) "Books, please." And that would be a request, a very polite request. Politer than many a request in this hard world. Only trouble: It requires a comma after "Books"— see, the Pedant has put it in—and there is none on the mobile. Nary a comma anywhere; Poofy just made a special trip into the hall to see. Surely the people who read books—and Poofy assumes that the mobile was made by people who read books although he cannot demonstrate this to be a fact —surely the people who read books would have known about that comma. Or maybe the rules have changed since you went to school, Mr. Pedant. Could be. We live in a world of change, so the books say.

Aw, forget the comma. Who makes the request for books? None of the people we have so carefully listed under No. 1: The cocktailer, the stormer at windows, the spreader of the word, the bridger, the golfer. Not even the lady fauceteer; well, perhaps she is the closest yet. But surely not the aesthete, the van packer, the politico, or the Pogo man—none of these guys. At least not all the time; probably not even a large part of the time.

Well, who *does* make the polite request?

"Books, please." *You* know. You hear it everywhere. In book stores and drug stores—only here, like the fauceteer, it is more apt to be "Book, please." In libraries, of course, you have heard the chorus; it is deafening: "Books, please, Books, please."

"Books, please." Who asks for books? Why, just look at the mobile. The two acrobats at the top with their waving mustaches; how do you suppose they learned to swing on the flying trapeze? Books, friend, books. The many muscled Samson beneath them; how do you think he ever learned to lift that great weight with only one hand ("Look, mom")? Books, of course. How else? The clown, how learned he clowning? The man with the whip, how learned he whipping? Out of books, friend. Probably books from the public library. Books from your friendly neighborhood library man.

Surely you remember out of your past: "Reading is the Key." The key to life, friend, and all the cushy jobs in life and all the fun and games in life and all the other treasures in Pandora's Box. Reading is the key and, of course, books please and all God's children cry "Books, please."

And yet. There was a time long, long ago, they say, when talking and seeing was the key. A time when Homer sang, and people flocked to see and hear plays. And there is a time right now when talking and seeing is the key. A time when boys and girls and men and women crowd around the black box to see and hear whether Mollie took up with that nice young man or that out-of-town character who means her no good at all.

And there is a time coming; it's later than you think. A time when you don't go to the book store or the drug store or the library or even the television set. You just go to that handy little console in your handy little home and punch this and that and fiddle with this and that and—lo, you have a printout. Maybe not as pretty as a book or a dame; but it's twice as useful—so they say.

And the sloganizer of the old time religion gives way to the sloganizer of the new fangled creed. He also says only two words:

"Consoles please."

Bra, Bra, Black Sheep

Mrs. Quirina Throttlebottom sailed majestically to the desk and her voice boomed over the library.

"My dear, I just adore your letter to the Editor of *Mac-Recalls* about their dreadful article on" (she lowered her shout to a whisper) "you know what."

Behind the desk Sabina Twiggle smiled demurely. "Oh, really, Mrs. Throttlebottom, it was nothing at all. I just did my duty as a good librarian always must be prepared to do it. After all, we are members of a great profession and just as a good doctor would never prescribe poison for his patients so we as librarians must never prescribe poison to our clients. Who knows what young mind might have been driven to evil thoughts—if not evil deeds—by that awful article? So I just took that issue off the shelf and wrote the letter. It was not much, really, but—"

"Oh, my dear, what on earth is *that?*" Mrs. Throttlebottom's pudgy finger swept down to Miss Twiggle's desk where the boy had just deposited the morning mail. Sabina looked and gasped.

"Why—why—I can't think why they ever did something like *that!* The *Library Journal* is going way out but this is even past way out."

"The *Library Journal!*" Mrs. Throttlebottom was horrified. "But, my dear, the boy has on no clothes at all and there is his" (her shout again melted into a whisper) "you know what and—why, bless me, he is doing his business right into the river. What in the world can *that* have to do with libraries?—"

"Lady, can you swallow your voice a bit? It's mighty hard to read with such a—"

Mrs. Throttlebottom swung round and blasted away: "Sam Squirttle, don't you 'lady' me! Man and boy, I've known you and I don't know much good yet."

Sam grinned. "OK, Quiry, can't you pipe down? I came here to read, not to gas off." Sam turned to Sabina: "Say, Sabby, what did you do with the last issue of *MacRecalls?* You know, the one you wrote that nasty letter about? I'd like to see it. I'm a manufacturer. Never can tell when I'd like to manufacture a bra." Sam's raucous voice boomed over the library quiet louder than Mrs. Throttlebottom's and he winked and grinned a wicked grin.

Sabina shrank. "Well—I guess it may still be in the safe. I was going to destroy it—"

"Destroy it!" Sam's anger blazed. "Why in blazes—"

"Now, Sam, stop that noise! Someone may be listening who could be injured by that article. Sabby is a professional just like a doctor. Sabby would never dream of prescribing poison—"

"Aw, pipe down, Quiry. I say it again, pipe down! Like a doctor, indeed! Prescribe indeed! What right has a nice little girl like Sabby to prescribe *anything* for me—let alone choose what I can and cannot read? Why, I'm twice as old as Sabby, and where did she get her six years' training like the doctor has? Even the doctor I don't let go too far. Like when he told me to lay off the bourbon. Imagine! Me! Lay off bourbon! So let's have the *MacRecalls*, Sabby, there's a good girl. After all, like I say, you never can tell when I may want to manufacture a—"

"Here it is, Mr. Squirttle." Sabby was glad to shut off the words. But she had cut him off only for a moment.

"There, that's better! No censorship here, by golly! Maybe you have a point about hiding it from kids—only maybe, I say, mind you! But you sure have no right to censor what adults read—and I'm sure Quiry here is an adult; she was born a month after me and I know. I reckon that makes me an adult too."

"Sam, do be still!" Quiry's boom shrank to a whisper. "Like you say, people come here to read."

Sam turned to go; then he swung around and confronted Mrs. Throttlebottom. "Hey, I almost forgot! What was all this fuss about a boy doing his business into the river?"

Sabina blushed. Mrs. Throttlebottom grabbed the *Library Journal* and thrust it into Sam's hand.

"That's what it is, you old rounder! Even you will have to admit that it is a sad day when a whole profession has to be exposed to a display like that!"

Sam laughed out loud. "Just like it used to be when I was a boy and we went swimming in Oskemawhoffee River. Those were the days!" His face clouded. "Boys can't do that today now that Job Throttlebottom has a factory there pouring its filth into the River." Sam smiled sweetly at Quiry. Absently he turned the pages; then he exploded. "Say! This is the real thing! This whole journal is about pollution! The boy is only an eye catcher. You know, Sabby, you librarians do a good job after all." He beamed and then he marched away with both magazines under his arm.

At the desk Mrs. Throttlebottom snorted. "Even so, my dear, I think you should tear off that cover if the old coot ever brings it back."

Cash and the Common Man

Dearly Beloved: This is a brief sermon on an ancient topic, and there are four texts all taken from the July 1967 issue of an ancient journal. The topic is professionalism (whatever that is) and the journal is *Library Journal* (whatever that is). There is also a fifth text from an ancient institution, Webster's Unabridged, second edition.

The first text, brethren and sisters, is on page 2502: "Maine Library Profile: Substandard Conditions." In this benighted state, so the text tells us, there are for public librarians no paid vacations, no sick leave, no pension, no salary schedule, no expenses for attending library meetings.

Is Maine a blessed state for the library professional? "No!" and a loud "Amen!" The chorus blasts the church walls. But, patience, my children; hear the second text on page 2536: A private firm employed by the Florida state legislature took a hard look at "work being done by academic library staff, and at the people doing the work" and announced in clarion notes that "all people working in academic libraries in Florida should be on clerical salary grades"; there is, indeed, "a very good chance that nobody in academic libraries in the state will now be classified as professional."

Again, fond flock, I ask: Is Florida a blessed state for the library professional? Another "No!" and another crashing "Amen!" But again, I beseech you, hold up that loud

"Amen." Hear the third text on page 2530: An "active consultant" suggested that the fees for consultants should be high because "Management won't listen to any consultant unless he costs $200 a day plus expenses"; and "a voice" replied that NLA should accredit consultants, "there being a lot of poorly qualified consultants running loose around the country."

A consultant, it seems, gets some cash—a lot of cash compared with what our dear brethren in Maine and Florida get for their kitties. Is a consultant a professional? Who knows? Forget not the words of "the voice." Hear now the fourth text from the same page: An "audience of about ten people" attended the "annual post mortem" on *Special Libraries*. They heard, among other things, a request for "more practical rather than theoretical articles" because "library schools are not teaching the application of theory needed by bread-and-butter . . . librarians," a request for abstracts of theses, an eager debate on what the cover of *SL* should look like and the decision that the cover need not be sexy because it is the duty of every professional to read his professional journal, no matter how dowdy. But most important of all was the "verdict that an editorial stand on such hot issues" as the "Florida matter" could not be taken "without official sanction from SLA's higher powers."

Is this a professional attitude toward a professional journal? "No" or "Yes" or "May be": how shout ye this time, my brethren? And what of the "Amen"?

"What *is* professional? Hear ye now at last the last text, Webster, Unabridged, second edition, definition no. 3: Professional is "engaging for livelihood or gain in an activty pursued, usually or often, for noncommercial satisfactions by amateurs; as a *professional* golf player; a *professional* soldier."

So cash is the key. Again no "Amen"? Only a dead silence? Perhaps a "Boo!"

O.K. Just take a look around you.

The amateur—the guy who does the work for nothing simply because he likes to do it—well, he is *only* an amateur; he is not a professional. This means, of course, the nice little old lady who runs the nice little old library in the nice little old home town for no nice little old reason at all more than that she loves books and likes to see people and talk to people about books. Of course! That's what she is—just an amateur. But the little old lady is not alone.

Look at the professional journals run by our library professional organizations. Their editors get no pay; they are lucky if they get some slight bit of cash to help with their expenses. Their contributors get no pay; they are lucky if they get reprints of their articles without having to pay the journal for them. (I have heard it whispered that even among the professional journals published to make money this is often true of the contributors; I speak naught of the editors of such journals.) Are these people professional or are they like the nice little old lady—simply amateurs who do what they do for "noncommercial satisfactions"?

For that matter, look at (and listen to or, more accurately, sit through) professional meetings and their professional speakers. How many of these speakers get cash for their (sometimes) thought-out words of (sometimes) wisdom? How many speak only for "noncommercial satisfactions"?

There is, of course, another side of this coin. Examine, pray, the *content* of professional journals. How many journals engage in (or even allow) discussion of controversial matters? Perhaps there is here, after all, a concern for cash— or at least a concern about giving offense to those who in some way might be a source of cash to the profession. On this point, then, journals are professional.

Now look at some of the other things said of *Special Libraries:* "Practical rather than theoretical articles"—this means easier ways to earn cash, so it is a professional consideration. Library schools and their failure with "bread-and-butter courses"—what thought could be cashier, i.e., more profesional? Abstracts of theses so you won't have to take time to read the darned things but you *can* get the extra cash their ideas may bring you—surely we have to call this professional. And take no thought for the cover of any library journal because sex and the common man are not as professional as cash and the common man, and how can you get more cash if you do not read your journal?

It seems, dear friends, that we shall have to call our journals professional after all—even if their editors and contributors do not qualify.

What of the elected officers and appointed committees of all the professional organizations which sponsor all these journals and meetings? Are they truly professional—in it for the cash they can get? Or are they only amateurs looking for "noncommercial satisfactions," amateurs who get the organization moving by means of handouts from other members' time and energy and all too often handouts from the institutions which allow employees to work for the professional association on company time?

What about the poor guys and dolls who labor in Maine and in Florida? They, dear brethren and sisters, are, after all, professionals. They work for cash instead of "noncommercial satisfactions." Only in one respect are they not professional: they attend professional meetings at their own expense, that is, they are amateurs who put out cash and energy to get to those meetings for "noncommercial satisfactions."

Who, then, is the "clerical"? Who is the "semi-professional"? Who is the "library technician"? No one, dear little flock, no one. They all get cash for what they do—except, of course, the dear little old lady with whom we began this discourse.

Finally, my brethren, what makes the professional? Cash is the answer, boy, the folding green stuff. And if we are to be logical—who does not want to be logical?—the more cash, the more professional. So who is the most fully professional of us all? Plain as the proverbial nose, my friends, plain as the proverbial nose. The most cash, the most professional. The administrators of large libraries, the consultants—of such is the Kingdom of Profession.

Continuum of Fog

On the week end of the great fog the committee climbed to the chairman's cabin high on Lookout Mountain to ponder the curriculum. For five hours they sat around the huge fireplace and nursed their drinks and stared into the bright flames. At last the chairman gave words to their meditations:

"The trouble is that we have been thinking all students can be prepared to work in any library by one general curriculum—"

"But, Chug, what's wrong with that notion?"

Simperson Chugon frowned. He did not like to be called "Chug" (although everyone did it); he did not like the word "notion" ("concept" was much better); and he did not care for Irv Decal's interruptions (the old fossil even believed in cataloging laboratories). But he dragged out a patient look.

"The trouble, Irv, is that this concept of the all-purpose curriculum means only that we have looked at all library operations in all libraries and then derived from these operations what we call general concepts or principles. For example, we think of the concept of collection development as a set of principles which could be applied in any library. We even say that our curriculum, involved with such concepts, is removed from the library as an institution and deals only with concepts and principles—not with details of everyday operations."

"That's right, Chug." Hilda Gagg nodded sagely. "Only yesterday one of our alumni was complaining that we are too theoretical; said it took three weeks to get our last graduate onto the track. Even said he would not want any more of our graduates."

"But, Hilly, he was all wrong." Chug somehow found Miss Gagg even more of a problem than Irv; Irv had at least kept on the track. "He was all wrong, Hilly, because our curriculum is not theoretical at all; we just *think* it is. What we call concepts in our curriculum are themselves only extrapolations of a great variety of library operations as I was saying. So in a very real sense our curriculum is operation-centered rather than concept-centered."

Hilly frowned: she was silenced but not convinced. Indeed, she was not sure she understood what Chug was talking about. Irv understood but he also was not convinced.

"Chug, what is a concept if it is not a way to deal with a fact? And what is dealing with a fact if it is not an operation? Can you even have the concept unless you have had to deal with the fact? For instance, can you have the concept of intellectual freedom if you have not had to deal with the fact of repression? For that matter, do you even *need* the concept if you do not have to deal with the fact? Of *course*, our concept-centered curriculum is actually operation-centered. So what else is new?"

Chug filled his pipe in silence. No use to argue with Irv. But the chairman could not really stay quiet long. He changed the subject:

"Suppose we conceptualize the audience as existing along a continuum. At the left end of the continuum one would find the always purposeful, all-consuming audience, very literate, communicating in a great variety of ways, critical and analytical, self-aware, self-confident, curious. At the other end of the continuum, the individual would be illiterate (or nearly so), seldom communicate, except perhaps orally, have a poor self-image, and be generally not curious."

"That sounds reasonable, Chug." Hilly could understand this and she shared Chug's love of "conceptualize" and "continuum." The words had a scholarly sound. The chairman smiled in triumph and moved on.

"Various forces in our society tend to press people to move from the right end of the continuum toward the left end. Various environmental factors, the educational system, mental energy of the individual, and any number of factors exert such pressure. Indeed, society grants both material and psychic rewards to the person who moves from right to left. Conceivably an over-riding objective of all institutions, including libraries and, therefore, library schools, would be to press the individual to move from right to left."

"But, sir, if I may interrupt." Chug turned with gladness to the student member; he liked to be called "sir" and he liked Hamilton Brasenose.

"Of course, Ham. We are glad to have the student point of view. What is it?"

"If I understand you correctly, sir, you are saying that society contains people who are literate and critical and people who are illiterate and uncritical and that society tends to push people from one extreme to the other."

"I suppose one could say it that way." Chug smiled indulgently; in time Ham would learn to use words like "continuum."

But just now Ham's mind was elsewhere. "But, sir, does society really encourage people to move from the extreme right to the extreme left? I suppose free schools and free libraries do help people become more literate and I suppose that to some extent society does offer what you call material and psychic rewards to people who become literate and most of those other things you were talking about. But does society often reward people for becoming critical and analytical? Does it not rather reward people if they stay somewhere in the middle of the 'continuum' as you called it, I believe?"

"Splendid," sang out Irv. "Ham, you are both literate and critical. You are at the left end of Chug's continuum for sure!"

Mrs. Simperson Chugon charged into the fireplace circle with offerings of drinks and cheese and cakes and many another such. The woman in Chug's life had never looked so good to him.

Chug began the morning of the second day of the fog with some objectives for the curriculum which he had drawn up after last night's meeting.

"First of all, I am sure, we shall agree that the curriculum should promote development of critical, analytical attitudes." Chug had explained to Ham last night that this was a good objective even if it might not always lead to reward, and the rest of the company was too tired of the subject to debate it this morning.

"Objective number 2: Provide future-oriented leaders."

"Hold up on that one, Chug!" The night's rest in the mountains had done wonders for Irv. "What's the great thing about being future-oriented? Hitler was future-oriented—1,000 years' worth. You are future-oriented; I am future-oriented; everyone is future-oriented or he is dead. It's the *kind* of future you are oriented to that matters."

"You are right, Professor Decal! You know, I had never thought of it that way. 'Future-oriented,' I guess is only jargon—oh, I'm sorry, sir!" Ham had just caught sight of Chug's face. "But, sir, you will have to admit that Professor Decal has a point." Forthright young man, noted Irv with smiling approval.

Chug moved quickly to Objective number 3: "Instill strong sense of ethics."

"That's a good point perhaps." Gilbert Storm spoke slowly as if he were thinking aloud. Then the idea sleeping in the back of his mind awoke. "But, Chug, just what do you mean by that objective? We have a Code of Ethics drawn up a long time ago by a batch of old time administrators and meaning almost nothing. Also we have each our own code of ethics—but there seems to be little wrong with the ethics of our students if Ham's remarks about 'future-oriented' mean anything. They have thoughtful opinions about the profession and they are willing to stand up for them."

"Gil, you have a good point there. Ham has no need for any of us to work on his ethics." Chug could be a gracious loser.

"Now about Objective number 4: Produce people who are at ease in varied situations."

"Well, sir, I'm not sure about that one." Ham had been encouraged by success. "It sounds a bit like a public relations gimmick. I am not so sure I should like to live with people who were at ease in varied situations. One thing has made this meeting interesting; you are not any of you at ease in the varied situations that arise. You each have a point of view and you each express it and you each gain or lose self confidence as your point rises or sinks in favor. You could hide your feelings, I suppose, but that would only make you phonies."

Mrs. Simperson Chugon called them to lunch. And so ended the week end of the great fog.

Digging up a Dean

In his roomy eighteenth century office the genial Provost stood by the huge fireplace and outlined the duties of the Committee to Nominate a Dean for the Library School. Then the Committee trudged back across campus to the shabby seminar room and pulled hard chairs to the rickety table.

The Chairman ran his fingers through his bushy white hair. "First of all, the Provost says we have to set up some criteria. Any suggestions?"

"He must be a man, not over fifty, and he must have a Ph.D." Augustus Crabthorn had never been called wishy-washy.

"Now, Thorny, you know quite well a woman could do just as good a job or better!" For lo these many years Olivia Spunkerei had talked and paraded for women's rights.

Thorny rose and bowed. "Yes, Olly, I suppose a woman could do as good a job as a man—maybe better. But would she? How many deans in the country are women?"

"That's exactly what I have in mind, Thorny. Mighty few deans are women. But that does not mean women can't be deans. It only means that male deans are the status quo. It only means women simply have not been given a chance. It's a matter of civil rights pure and simple. Sex is no better way to discriminate than color. The School has a splendid chance to make a significant contribution to the movement for women's rights if we choose a woman for a dean."

Thorny grinned. "OK, Olly, OK. You have made your point. There are few women deans because it is a man's world. And in a man's world, my dear, women will work more smoothly for men than men will work for women. You have made your point, Olly, and in making it you have proved that we need a man for dean."

"Much as I hate to say it, I'll have to agree with Professor Crabthorn." Gayel Leggers was the youngest member.

"Thank you, Gayel. Thank you much." Thorny liked Gayel. She was bright and she was good to look upon.

"Gayel, dear, do you really agree with Thorny? Or is it simply that you would rather work for a man dean than for a woman dean?" Olly was not noted as a diplomat.

Thorny laughed aloud. "Olly, you have proved my point beyond a doubt."

Olly flushed a bit in spite of herself and the rest of the Committee smiled.

The Chairman broke into the silence: "Let's get on to your next idea, Thorny: Not over fifty. Anybody object?"

"The Age of the Young and Beautiful." Cordelia Golroy sighed. "It is the fashion to exalt the young just as it is the fashion to exalt the men. Is it really more than a fad? What of the wisdom that comes with experience?"

"But, Cordy, does wisdom really come with experience? Or is that notion just a bit of folklore—a fad of our generation?" Thorny spoke slowly; he was not himself entirely sure of this age business. "There's no fool like an old fool." Somehow repeating the adage gave him comfort.

"Unless he's a young fool," snapped Olly. "Just look at what's happening at Gabbelgate. There's a young dean for you! He's a man too! That School will do well to keep its doors open let alone get National Library Association accreditation."

"But, Olly, under fifty does not mean he has to be only twenty-five. It means only that he would be able to welcome new ideas and able to have time to carry them out before retirement."

"If that's what you want, Thorny, then why not make it at least fifty-five? That's not dead old, you know."

"Mr. Chairman, I defer to the wisdom of age." Again Thorny rose and bowed to Olly. "Let's make it under fifty-five."

Olly scowled, but they all agreed and the Chairman moved ahead:

"What about Thorny's last big idea: Must be a Ph.D.?"

"I can not see that as valid." George Gabbertin was the next to the youngest member. "I belong to that union myself and I suppose it would help to have a Ph.D. for dean but as an absolute requirement—no."

"Why not, Gabby? Why be a traitor to your class?" James Bean had proudly borne the title for twenty years; even his stationery flaunted it.

"Beano, you'll have to admit that a Ph.D. doesn't mean anything necessarily about what a man can really do."

"Well, I don't know—" Beano fell silent. In twenty years he had written two reviews.

"Well, I know!" Thorny snapped into the breach. "To be a Ph.D. means that a man has had the self discipline to go through with a long and arduous task; it means he has developed scepticism; it means he has been creative enough to write something that adds to the knowledge or to the understanding of mankind. It means he is committed to the life of scholarship, the life of scepticism, the life of creative writing. He may, it is true, not live up to that commitment." (Thorny dared not look at Beano.) "But that commitment and its promise are there just the same."

"Bravo, bravo!" Gabby clapped his hands in mockery. "Sure, Thorny, sure! A wee bit of melodrama but sure anyway. But you don't *have* to be a Ph.D. to be all those things. Just look at Lanny Crisby in Cracklebury School, for instance."

"OK, just take a look at Lanny. What's to see?"

Gabby was aghast. "What's to see? Everything, that's what! Why, just look at what he's done. Made surveys all over the country. Written articles in library periodicals. Director of Pudge City Library for years. Vice President of NLA—what more do you want?"

"What more do I want?" Thorny was pensive. "Why, nothing I guess, Gabby—nothing more than a Ph.D. Lanny has made a career out of getting his. Started in fifteen years ago. Never bothered to finish up. Too busy making surveys. Too busy writing flashy, fluffy stuff in *Library Journal*. Too busy knowing the right people in NLA."

Gabby sputtered. "Now you are being unfair and you know it. Why Lanny—"

"Oh, let's forget Lanny; he's not on our agenda." The Chairman was growing weary.

"Right!" Thorny was angry but his voice was soft. "This school is starting a Ph.D. program next year. To be more exact, we shall be asking for one. The Provost and the Dean of the Graduate School are Ph.D.'s—Ph.D.'s of the old school: Humanities and all that jazz. What chance do you think we have if we propose a Ph.D. program to be run by a non-Ph.D.? For that matter, what credibility will we have in the profession—if you will pardon the word—with a non-Ph.D. running our Ph.D. program. And we can't claim it is because they are so scarce. With things going as they are, Ph.D.'s will be a dime a dozen in five years."

"So much for Thorny's three points." The Chairman was relieved but he was not through. "I propose a point myself: The dean should not be a library administrator."

Everyone gasped.

"And just why, may I ask, do you say that?" Olly had

once run a university library. Did a good job too, so they had told her.

"I know why." Thorny would not wait for the Chairman. "An administrator has to decide things—a thousand things a day. He can't wait to think them through; he has to decide them now. But the more he knows about a problem the better he will see the two sides and the better both sides will look. Neither side will be white; neither will be black; both will be gray. In short, dear Olly, the better his brain and the more he knows the poorer he will be as an administrator. Now to be a dean—"

"Oh, come off it, Thorny!" The Chairman grinned but he did not want Olly to turn stubborn just now. "What you say may be true, Thorny, but it really is not all that bad. The chief reason why we don't want an administrator is that a dean's job is different. If an administrator does not like what his catalog department is doing he can tell the head cataloger to change it or get another job. But a dean now: He has to deal with cranky people like us—people who have tenure and our own ideas and our own little ways of getting what we want. I'm sure Olly doesn't want some bossy dean coming in and telling her how to run her A-V courses."

Olly smiled. "Right you are, Mr. Chairman. Right you are. But one thing bothers me about all this talk. We have competition. Half the schools in the country are looking for deans. The Provost can talk his head off about criteria. But first we have to find someone who wants the job."

The Chairman nodded. "Digging up a dean is like digging up a mummy. You may know exactly what kind of specimen you want but you end up glad to get what you can find."

Earthshaker at Ease

The plane mounted high and the young man at the window watched Oceanic City fade away far below. He unbuckled his seat belt and sank back. Suddenly he was tired and with a shock he realized that this was the first time in a week there was no meeting to go to, no plans to make, no midnight debate to share. It was something to sit and listen to the motor.

He smiled in contentment. What a glorious week it had been. How much they had got done. Who would have dreamed in those chaotic first hours . . . ? He fished the worn paper from his pocket and unfolded it on his lap. Lazily he began to read it once more.

"Our time for commitment to action is at hand." And so it had been. The NLA Establishment had at last been made to hear from them. It would not be the last they would hear.

"We are losing our public because we are indifferent to their needs, and we are losing the dignity of our positions." A tiny doubt stirred in the back of his mind. Was that really why his library was losing its public—or had the public just moved away? Had he really been indifferent to the new public's needs or had he tried to understand those needs and failed? For that matter what was this "dignity of our positions"? Had librarians ever truly had it? He stared out into the light blue sky and the fleecy clouds. Then he came back to the paper. "Our responsibility is to return to the basic

meaning of library service." A nice sentiment with a noble
ring—but what did it mean? What was this "basic meaning"?

Absently he paid the pretty girl for the bourbon and
settled back to enjoy it. After a long while his eyes came
back to the paper still in his lap.

"The times are changing; we MUST change with them.
Unless we respond to the challenge of our times, we will
become useless." Even back in Oceanic City when they had
debated, the caps in "MUST" had seemed a bit melodra-
matic, and the whole two sentences had seemed a little too
obvious. But he had not objected. After all, the truth always
seems trite if you think of it.

"Our only present solution is to mobilize, organize . . ."
His doubts faded. Here, at last, he was on firm ground.
This *was* the only solution in the crisis. Mobilize and
organize:

"To accept our moral responsibility to commit ourselves
to social and political issues such as war, poverty, and
racism." He read it again, this time slowly. Precisely what
did the line mean? What they had *intended* was clear:
They meant that librarians should stand *against* war, poverty, and racism. They meant that libraries should stand
against war, poverty, and racism. But was that what they
had said? "To commit ourselves" did not mean for or
against. What did "commit" mean? Censorship? Only
anti-war, anti-poverty, anti-racism books in the library? And
whose anti-war? The President's or the Senator's? Uneasily
he moved to the next line:

"To commit ourselves to the restructure of the National
Library Association into a democratic and vital organization." The NLA President was a good guy. He had been
real friendly when the young man presented him the letter
J. B. had written. And he and the incoming President had
been thoughtful and sympathetic at the meetings when

they had presented their demands. And there was this new Committee on the NLA the new President would appoint with some of their representatives on it. Perhaps the young man would himself be appointed; after all, there was J. B.'s letter to the outgoing President. That committee would be an interesting assignment . . . Maybe NLA was not such a mess after all . . .

"To commit ourselves to reform the structure and content of library education." The young man had not been so sure about this one as the kids in school now. He had himself gone to a good school; he had since served in the alumni association. Oh, sure, there were some courses which he had never needed, some profs who had not been in libraries lately, but was it really any worse than it had been in high school and college? He moved to the next line.

"To commit ourselves to take action in support of librarians in cases where job security and professional integrity are threatened." This had bothered him a bit: "To take action." What kind of action? It would have to be something more than moral support if it meant anything. Was NLA—even under new management—about to give more than moral support? The week had given him little hope here. And should jobs always have "security" regardless of what their possessors did? And what was "professional integrity"? The NLA Code of Ethics would not answer that one clearly. They would have to do some more work on this statement. He moved on.

"To commit ourselves to the community's participation in determining the services which are relevant to it." Splendid; perhaps one of the best of the commitments. And yet now that he read it again, how would the community participate? By voting? A lot of time and trouble and expense there. By the voices of its leaders? Who were the community's leaders? The local Martin Luther Kings or the local Rap Browns? The local Agnews or the local Lindsays?

The young man remembered too that community participation in determining large city school services had not been always completely successful. And what about cost? How would that fit in with the library system concept?

"To commit ourselves to the restructure of library administration to insure that library workers have a voice in decisions that affect them." This he had gone along with because some of his new-found friends said it was needed. The young man had no problems in his own library; in fact, J. B. had given him the money for his expenses to Oceanic City. He liked J. B.; only two weeks ago J. B. had promised him the assistant librarianship if Jakby left.

"To commit ourselves to the formation of a national union of library workers." This also, the young man had endorsed because they told him it was necessary in some libraries. At home J. B. himself was already working on the idea of a union in the Library.

"Finally, to reaffirm our total commitment to library service and to every individual's right to free access to information." He moved uneasily. There it was again: "library service." And again with no clearcut idea as to what it meant. "Free access to information": This was clear enough. But shouldn't it have come sooner in the statement? And was it only a statement or would someone somehow enforce it? Certainly the new NLA—even under pressure—had not done much to reassure him in Oceanic City. "Free access to information." There had been ugly stories in Oceanic City about people who had lost their jobs for holding to the idea and he had idly wondered how he would stand the test. After all, there were Margy and little Sue . . . "Free access to information." This had not changed. It had always been an ideal in libraries. Why hadn't it come first?

The light flashed: "Fasten your seat belts." Over the loud speaker boomed the pilot's voice: "We are landing . . ."

Featherstone Among the Amazons

Featherstone has a problem. It began long before he was born. 1856 was the year and Mrs. A. B. Harnden was the name. For the very first time in the history of the world a woman hired out her services (non-professional) to a librarian. His name was William Frederick Poole and his library was the already hallowed Boston Athenaeum.

All of this even he who runs may read in that grab bag of library bits and pieces *Bowker Annual*, 1968, p. 310. But only he who stops to meditate will grasp the awesome meaning of 1856.

Ghosts of libraries past and souls of libraries present from Assurbanipal's Ninevah to the British Museum must have groaned. True, women were not new; they had been there all the time. Callimachus was a poet and even in the heart of so wooden a poet there surely lurked a tiny warm corner for women. Antony, so some say, gave Pergamum's library to Cleopatra. Queen Christina of Sweden took her library to Rome. The Reverend Thomas James had to wait a whole year till Sir Thomas Bodley would let him marry. Casanova became a librarian in the end. Always there had been women in the lives of libraries and librarians. But for a woman to work in a library somewhere not at the end of a mop! This was another kettle of fish.

Mr. Poole did not confine his attentions to one woman. Exactly twenty years later, then in the Chicago Public Library, he wrote about "ladies in the eastern cities" (ever present sources of the new and dangerous) whose "services can be temporarily secured" for cataloging and who are "also skilled in library management." Frederick William would, indeed, "be happy to furnish to any committee [why only to a committee?] the names and addresses of several ladies who are not surpassed in the qualifications for such work" (*Public Libraries in the United States*, 1876, part 1, p. 490).

The disease was contagious. In this same big book (p. 430) F. B. Perkins of the Public Library of Boston (one of Mr. Poole's "eastern cities") announced that "women should be employed as librarians and assistants as far as possible, as the nature of the duties is, to a great extent, and in many cases, suited to them." There were, he confessed, some drawbacks. For heavy work you would have to fall back on men. Even worse there are "curious troubles arising from the fact that women in such places often do not get along with other women as well as men do," although "supervisory authority" can, of course, solve this "friction by admonition, or, if necessary, by a change in the service."

Of the 104 librarians who attended the first ALA meeting in 1876 only 13 were women. But today Mr. Poole's little black book has swollen to a massive annual paperback called *ALA Membership Directory*. If you look hard you will find a few non-female names lurking here and there—corporate bodies and male bodies. But only 2 out of 10 librarians are men. And this is Featherstone's problem! He is one of those two guys. Behind every plumber you will find perhaps a wife and perhaps a mother and perhaps a daughter or two and perhaps even a secretary. Behind Featherstone you will find all these but also you will find a harem.

It is just like they say it with music in the little black box: "You've come a long way, baby, to get where you are today, baby. You've come a long, long way." Yes indeed. With non-library men it is not so. Holders of 60 per cent of the jobs in all professional and technical occupations are men. In 1964 of all physicians 4 per cent were women; of all scientists 8 per cent; of all engineers 1 per cent. Even in social work and secondary school teaching there were more men than women. At this point the National Advisory Commission on Libraries waxes pontifical and ponderous: "As is true of most professions in which women predominate at the lower and middle levels . . . the prestige of librarianship as a whole is lower in the public view than it deserves to be, and the financial rewards are less tempting than in many other professions . . ." (*ALA Bulletin*, January 1969, p. 84). You see where that leaves Featherstone. How can he escape this matriarchy, this kingdom of the Amazons?

The answer rings clear as a bell. Featherstone must get a cushy grant and make a plushy study. Blow up a whirlwind of questionnaires. Better yet, he can hop a plane and go and see all these pretty little old woman in their pretty little old mini-skirts. He should find out everything first hand; there is really nothing quite the same as an expert man's (or even a non-expert man's) face-to-face visit with a woman. How did Featherstone and that other guy fall into this trap? Just because Mrs. A. B. Harnden once hired out to William Frederick is no excuse for Featherstone's predicament. How can Featherstone get out of the trap? (Does he really want out?) Featherstone will enjoy the grant; the women will enjoy Featherstone. Even more important, he will come up with a thick book with his name on the cover. Featherstone may even come up with an answer; but normally that is not required of a study.

There is only one problem: The study has already been done. Where did you think I dredged up all those juicy

statistics? Done by a woman, alas; it cannot have been half
the fun Featherstone would have had. Done by a good
looking girl (if we may believe the ever-present *LJ* picture)
named Anita R. Schiller, and she calls her little report in
LJ, March 15, 1969 (1098-1100) "The Widening Sex Gap."
Maybe you had not noticed the gap, but it is not that kind
of gap. She drags in some more statistics. Seems that not
one of the 50 largest academic libraries in the U.S.A. is
headed by a woman. Perhaps that is because of the "curious
troubles" Mr. Perkins complained about? Seems that when
men and women do the same kind of library work the
woman's salary is even more measly than the man's. Dis-
crimination, that's what. Featherstone is not just in a trap;
he is a mean old skunk. If you want the grisly details you
can go and read the Schiller book; but the taste of this *LJ*
sample is enough to show that the study idea is out. Out,
that is, if Featherstone wants an answer; but not out, of
course, if all he wants is a grant so he can have enough
cash to go and see a batch of dames.

What to do?

Featherstone could take to the streets. That is the now
thing to do. Rise, ye working men of the library world.
Kick out all the women—or at least half of them. But would
men really like that? And who would take the women's
jobs? Men who would work at women's salaries? Men
would not like that either. Rise, ye working men of the
library world; rise and strike; that is a thing even more now.
That would suit the administrators because they could fill
the jobs with mini-skirted scabs at three-fourths the price.
Of course, the administrators would themselves be women
working at three-fourths the price. And *they* would not like
that. Anyway, where would all the men go? After living in
a world of women for so long, how long would Featherstone
last in a world of men like physicians and scientists and
engineers?

Perhaps the only thing left for Featherstone is an ALA Men's Auxiliary, a tiny beachhead to hold some little while against the onrush of femininity.

Alas, poor Featherstone, we knew him well.

Fire and Pill

You have heard of the Great Mini Machine? Of course, you have if you are an up and comer. Anyway, this Great Mini Machine (just in case you have not heard of it after all) can put a library of 20,000 volumes on one (just one, mind you) 8 x 10 inch piece of nickel or aluminum foil. And then you can store it away for one hundred (100) years with no fuss or bother about humidity or temperature.

Just like the squirrel and the nut.

And that is how the machine solves the book explosion. Simple, direct action. Make the book smaller. 20,000 on one little 8 x 10.

In the old days we were content with even simpler great devices for the book explosion. Remember that magnificent fire at Alexandria? But who wants to be old fashioned? Get with it, friend. You're in the Pepsi generation. You have the machine.

Only problem with the minibook: Offhand, can you name 20,000 books that ought to be kept around for 100 years?

But this is really a miniproblem: The answer is obvious. Get a grant from the Council on Library Resources. In palmier days we might have called in the Feds as well. Our lobby had once trained them to think that books count. We could have chanted a new theme: Books Count for Little. But now the Feds say the cash is gone—even for

Little. This is no time to think less than big about the minibook.

Then use all that money to set up Standards. (By all means let us have Standards.) And the rest will be easy. We shall divide all books by the length of time they deserve to be preserved. Of some books we shall say: Destroy immediately. Of others: Keep a year. Of others: Keep 100 years. Of still others: Keep 1000 years. Et cetera and et cetera. The Standards will tell you.

And that is the end of the book explosion; worry no more about it. You can sleep again at nights (or any other time if you insist).

But can we keep this great discovery to ourselves and our own little explosion? Librarians—you will find it written in the books and the skies and shouted from the housetops and the library schools—Librarians are not good librarians if they are not socially useful. Librarians must bring salvation to all mankind.

And what is mankind's biggest problem? The population explosion, of course.

All we need do is haul in that machine again. Minimize us. The man half an inch tall is just around the corner. And then there will be room for all of us—even the librarians, useful or not. And this population explosion's bang also will be a bust—a quiet minibust.

Just think of all the money we shall save. Minimen in minihouses in minicities of the living and minicities of the dead; minibooks in minilibraries; minithis in minithat. Think of all the books you can buy with all that multicash you save. Think of all the multiland to expand into—every miniman with his own minifigtree.

Of course, the miniman will have a tough struggle dragging out that 8 x 10 piece of foil if he ever wants to de-store it.

But we have forgotten our old friend the machine. When

you are a miniman forget not the machine. Call on the machine and all the knowledge of the world will be laid out before your minibrain.

You will have to know which 8 x 10 you want and which minibook on the 8 x 10—or will you? Surely the machine will have taken care of that too. It may be that someone will have to have instructed the machine. Perhaps, like Camelot, there will always be a Cataloger. But he can be minimized after he has done the job.

Hold up a minute. Call in the Council on Library Resources again. We need a management analysis with a lot of charts and figures and tables printed beautifully on beautiful paper. No doubt the charts and things will show us that with all the money we shall save when we are all minimen and miniwomen, it will be cheaper just to have a lot of extra copies of every book. Then on that 8 x 10 we can have one copy wherever anyone might look for it whether he is Deweyite or Colonite or in between. Maybe we do not need that Cataloger after all.

Miniman and Minibook: the Library of the World can be in your kitchen corner. And all the men and women of the world can live in your house. Nice.

There is no end to it. Suppose minibooks and minipeople multiply again into explosion. Shall we have to set a limit for people as we did with books? Of course not. All we have to do is increase the ratio of reduction . . .

And now all we need is someone to volunteer for experimental minification.

Who wants to be the first man—or woman—in mini? The line forms to the right.

But do not look at me, friend. I am a conservative and I am content with the good old way for dealing with explosions: Fire and the Pill.

Fresh Eggs Anyone?

Throgmorton tossed the *Library Journal* on the table and beamed at his wife. "Quin, you know, it's mighty fine to be a librarian. It's a profession so completely dedicated to serving the user."

"Why do you insist on calling it a profession, dear?" Quinta carefully threaded her needle and then picked up the sock with the big hole. Why were Throggy's big toes so long?

Throgmorton's face lighted with the holy light. "Because it *is* a profession. Just like the doctor, just like the lawyer, the librarian serves people."

"How do you mean that, Throggy?" Quin surveyed the big hole. Just what strategy to use in closing it?

"You see, dear, it's all a matter of needs. The doctor's client needs to be cured; the lawyer's client needs to win his case at law; the librarian's client needs to read. In each profession the practitioner answers the need of his client."

"Would you say also, Throggy, that the grocer serves the need of his client who needs to eat?" Swiftly she began to sew. She had found a strategy for Throggy's toe's hole and she thought she had found a strategy for Throggy's enthusiasm's hole.

"Why, I suppose you would." Throggy was taken back. Grocer indeed!

"Maybe jobs come in pairs like socks." Thoughtfully Quin watched the big hole turn little.

"How do you mean, dear?" Throgmorton spoke slowly; where was she leading him?

"Well, let's look at your doctor and your lawyer as a pair and your librarian and my grocer as a pair. Each pair answers the needs of its users—or clients if you prefer the word. The doctor and the lawyer decide what their clients need even though what they decide may not be what the clients want. The doctor may prescribe a diet and the lawyer may advise his client to confess."

"So?" Throgmorton was still in an uneasy fog.

"So how about the other pair? The librarian and the grocer give their clients what they want even though they may know that this is not what their clients need. If the fat man wants a pie, a pie is what he gets; if the boy flunking chemistry wants a sports story, a sports story is what he gets." The big hole was gone and she reached for the next sock.

Throgmorton slumped in his chair, but he managed a sheepish grin. "Ok, you win on that one, Quin. But where does it get you in the long run? Your example may just be an exception."

Quin deftly inserted the needle in the next sock; this hole was not so big. "Well, let's look at another thing about these two pairs. The grocer and the librarian deal in wares. Their chief concern is to choose wares their customers— that is, clients—will want; to display those wares where their clients will be attracted to them; and to arrange those wares so that they can find them quickly when they want them. The doctor and the lawyer have no wares to display; they deal in services."

"Ah, but that's where you're wrong, dear." Throgmorton grinned; triumph after all!

"How so?" Quinta calmly closed the little hole. She picked up another sock.

"Well, for one thing, my love, when the librarian chooses books, when he displays them attractively, and when he arranges them so that he can find them easily again—when he does all these things he also is performing services. What's more, you are forgetting all the services the librarian performs when he serves as reference librarian." Throgmorton grinned again.

Quinta quietly put the red thread through the needle again and began work on another hole. Why were Throggy's heels so sharp? Then she turned again to look at Throggy.

"I suppose you have something there, dear. The grocer shows the client where the baby food is shelved and the librarian helps the client find out when and how to mix the baby food with goat milk—"

"Oh, come now, Quinta! That's not really quite a fair way to put it, and you know it!"

"Of course not, dear." She smiled sweetly. "There *are* other questions, like when the librarian helps the client find out who is Zambosia's ambassador to Rangoonia even if the appointment was made only the day before."

Throgmorton winced; he wished he had not told her so triumphantly of his accomplishment last week. Quinta kept on smiling and kept on talking.

"Another thing about services. When the doctor and the lawyer perform their services they draw upon a special and specific fund of organized knowledge which they have taken four years or so to acquire and which they must add to every day. When the grocer and the librarian perform their services they draw on intuition, pragmatism, and whatever they may have learned about their clients' wants. The librarian does have to go to school for a year, but the content of what he gets in that year is not special and specific; it is whatever his particular school was offering that particular year."

Throgmorton squirmed. He reached for the *Library Journal*; but Quinta kept on.

"And that's not all about services. The doctor and the lawyer perform their services within the framework set by their training, their experience, their profession and their judgment; the grocer and the librarian perform their services within the framework of their training, their experience, their profession, and their bosses' decisions. Unless, of course, the grocer and the librarian happen to be the bosses themselves."

Throgmorton's socks' holes were all finished. So was Throgmorton.

Hand Out to the Has Beens

For two years Figgsby was a Shaper of Destiny, one of the giants in the land. And now that he is again a Nobody, he can still sit in the warm sunshine of Memory. Real consolation in these days when automation has climbed into his lap and the bomb is just around the corner. Oblivion tomorrow maybe, but at least Figgsby has had his Day.

You see, for two years he was a full and honored member of PEBCO (Program Evaluation and Budget Committee of the National Library Association) than which what could be whicher? To sit on this Committee and pass judgment on every little act in every little corner of the NLA Empire on which the sun sets never. To decide whether to grant the request of the ALD (Auxiliary Library Division) for an extra $50.00 so that the Division could publish that pamphlet on Library Auxiliaries for which folks have been panting from Singapore to Zanzibar. The agony of debating what may affect the future of the whole library world, and the ecstasy of deciding on $75.00 instead to ADLD (Advantaging Disadvantaged Librarians Division). Then comes the impassioned plea from ALD which earns good old ALD $25.00 (but *not* $50.00) taken from the budget of CUPLA (Committee for Upgrading Library Associations). There is, dear reader, nothing like it.

Of course, along with such soul-rending matters Figgsby and the PEBCO gang did have fun and games. At Midwinter they came two days before most people showed up; but that is the penalty of all destiny shaper types in our society which moves ever more toward shifting working hours from the shoulders of hoi polloi to the shoulders of the thinker. For two days they sat in solemn conclave and debated the program of the Association. There was one minor problem: Even with two whole days they could not begin to look carefully at the entire program. There was just too much looking for any one body—even so mighty and so thoughty a body as PEBCO—to keep tab on everything. So, faced by this lack of time and (I only whisper it) ability to deal with the Whole Thing, Figgsby's Leader must cook up something else to keep him busy.

For Figgsby's first Midwinter on PEBCO each member arose and told what he thought of NLA and its work and its prospects and whatever else might happen to come to his mind—hopefully a joke at which hopefully his colleagues would laugh. Some few brash souls ventured to suggest that NLA is a stick-in-the-mud—only they phrased it more gently somewhat thus: "NLA is sometimes too devoted to the status quo." There followed murmurs of outrage and even an attempt to get the remarks removed from the minutes. But the Chairman, brave man, indeed, allowed the dissidents to have their say and to have it recorded.

All of these wonderful things are now here recorded thus faithfully and in such detail because PEBCO in its great wisdom and driven by its great fear that hoi polloi might not really understand nor fully appreciate nor long remember anyway what had been said there—for these or for divers other worthy reasons PEBCO voted not to distribute its minutes to said polloi.

The second Midwinter was another story. This time, PEBCO talked only of one tiny corner of NLA's far-flung activities: The international scene. Every past president of a division who could find some sort of an excuse to do so—

and some who could not find much of a sort—got up and flung-far his division's glorious accomplishments in international relations and if there had been none in the past, he promised something Really Great for his division's foreign scenic work in the future—however dim and distant. Nor could Figgsby forget the panel: Four past presidents of NLA talked together about NLA and foreign prospects.

And thus each year PEBCO gave two whole days before Midwinter to program evaluation and the members all came forth truly better and wiser men and women. Budget was another matter. At each Midwinter PEBCO elected three of its members to sit between Midwinter and the summer convention with a select committee well weighted with NLA's *Biggest* Shapers of Destiny and draw up a budget.

Then two days before hoi polloi gathered for the summer convention, Figgsby's happy little in-group met again. They had the grim facts of cash available and how much each division wanted laid before them and they decided who got the extra $25.00 or (much more often) who had to give it up because there would simply not be that much loot left if NLA kept its commitments to the Library Association of St. Slamius Island, and made sure that there was a copy of *Fanny Hill* in every library in the country. At last deliberations ended and the select committee met apart from the more lowly Shaper types; and then the lowly ones all came back again to approve the work of the select committee. PEBCO had done its duty to God and man and country and good old NLA and they went on their way rejoicing to all those fascinating meetings sandwiched in between the cocktail hours.

And that, dear readers, is the true story of how Figgsby helped save the country in his finest hour. Who were his colleagues? Well, there were three members at large, the NLA president, the NLA president-elect, the NLA treasurer

—and the NLA immediate past president (who acted as Chairman) and the immediate past presidents of the divisions, each accompanied by his executive secretary to guide him through the ordeal to no harm. Also present were the necessary other members of the executive secretariat.

Who were the members of PEBCO? They were the has beens, dear reader, only the has beens. Something a feller must have to let him gently down and out in the year after his breath-taking year on the summit as president of this or that. So NLA had PEBCO—hand out to the has beens.

And that is why NLA was once such a great and groovy gang. But now evil days have come and PEBCO is itself a has been. Or so they say.

Hearing is Believing

She was young and bright and good looking and she smiled a sweet smile. "Dr. Grankshaw, why did you put that red mark there?" She pointed to the first of many red marks on her paper.

"You mean you really don't know?" The Professor was horrified. Miss Manymede was still young and bright and good looking and she still smiled a sweet smile—but . . .

"No sir, I really don't know." The smile froze a bit. What was wrong with the old guy anyway?

"Well, you have spelled it 'possibley,' Miss Manymede." The big eyes widened. "What's wrong with that, sir?"

"Possibly has no 'e.' "

"Oh, is that all? I was afraid it was something important."

"But it is important, Miss Manymede. You have written a very good paper, but it is full of misspelled words. That's what all the red marks are for."

"I suppose you're right." She frowned; then she brightened. "But you understood what I meant, sir. Isn't that all that counts really?"

"Of course, I understood what you meant, Miss Manymede. But the words are still misspelled."

"But, Dr. Grankshaw, is spelling relevant in today's multimedia world? Sight and sound mean a lot more than how to spell. You can always get clerical help to clean up the misspelling in what you write when you do have to write something. Besides in the real world you'd probably dictate it anyway."

"The spelling did not affect your grade, Miss Manymede. As I said, it is a good paper—a bit wordy perhaps but on the whole a good paper."

"But, Dr. Grankshaw, loads of people can't spell. They say Robert Frost couldn't spell."

"You are not Robert Frost. Anyway, Frost was hardly an audio-visual enthusiast. Indeed, I suppose we should have to call him something in the humanities—if one may use that word in a multimedia age."

She shifted the attack. "But, sir, the Age of Gutenberg is over. So is the Age of Webster—Webster's dictionary and Webster's spelling book. Librarians must adjust to this new multimedia age even if they have always worked only with books in the past. If we don't adjust to progress we shall be left behind and the media specialists will take over the job we should be doing. The medium is the message, sir." She smiled brightly.

"And if the medium is full of misspellings that too is a message within a message." Dr. Grankshaw smiled himself.

Miss Manymede was undaunted. She shifted again: "Why learn how to spell any more than how to show a batch of slides or run a movie machine? Any clerk can do that. Librarianship is a profession, not a batch of deadly clerical routines."

"Let's stick to your media, Miss Manymede." Dr. Grankshaw was a bit bored with all talk about professions. "Let's stick to media—or as some of you have it, materials. Just what do you have in mind when you talk of medium?"

Miss Manymede swallowed. "Well, you know. Anything that carries a message—you know, like a film or a record or a picture or a slide or you know . . ." Her voice trailed off.

"Or a book?" Dr. Grankshaw's voice was gentle. "A book

carries a message. And it also has a lot of shapes. Clay tablet, papyrus roll, codex, microfilm, movie—what not?"

Miss Manymede had recovered. "But, sir, you will have to admit this is the age of the picture and the spoken word rather than the written and printed word only."

"Something like the age of Aristophanes and Socrates." His voice was still gentle. "You are correct, Miss Manymede. The medium carries a message. It is a record. And we are the keepers and the sharers of that record with others. Call us what you will. There will always be work for us—at least as long as there are records."

Miss Manymede had many virtues; listening to philosophical lectures was not one of them.

"Dr. Grankshaw, you win. Let's get back to spelling. I want to work in the library in the city. People in the ghetto can't spell. Many can't even read or use good English. Why shouldn't librarians speak and write as ghetto people speak and write if they want to be of service to them? Surely they will accept us more easily if we do."

"But you are not a ghetto product, Miss Manymede. Be what you are. As you young people say it: Do your own thing. You'll come across better than if you are a phony."

Miss Manymede's mouth fell open. The old guy was maybe all right?

"But I'd be a phony if I spelled correctly."

"As much a phony as if you let your secretary spell correctly for you."

Hints to the Harried

Does your boss bug you? Of course he does. You are only human.

You *can* bug him back. But, for Pete's sake, friend, don't do it. Your boss is human too—just like you. Well, at least it seems possible that he was born just as you were. (He may even have been a beautiful baby.) And (hopefully) he will die some day just as you will. Even if you cannot believe he is human, you can at least act as if you think he is. Like every human, he has his needs, and you are one of those needs. How could he be a boss if there were no bossed? So from cradle to grave your boss is your responsibility. Smooth the poor guy's journey from one to the other.

It is simple. Just remember the Five Laws of Library Administration you learned in graduate library school. Actually, there are two sets of five each. Check it with the Sage of the East: "Energy may manifest itself in one and the same subject more than once . . . The Second Manifestation of Energy is called Second Round Energy." So there are Five Laws of Library Administration (First Round); they are for your boss. And there are Five Laws of Library Administration (Second Round); they are for you.

Five Laws of Library Administration (First Round)

1. *Rock the Boat.*

Your boss has to change what the boss before him did. Maybe the old boss was doing what was right, but who can prove it now? Anyway, why do they need your boss if he keeps on doing only what the old boss was doing? So he's got to rock that boat. This makes real drama; it shows the boss is alive. It shows he is a go-getter. It shows he does too care about giving *better* service.

2. *Keep Rocking.*

One decisive action speaks louder than 1000 deliberations. So the boss must do something more; he must rock that boat again. What he does may be wrong or stupid. Chances are it is both. But so what? Remember the Third Law.

3. *Keep on Rocking.*

The boss has to go through at least one new administrative act every day. Perhaps two a day if he can think of them. He must practice acting; he must keep on acting. He must be a Man of Action. Then the critics of what he did yesterday will be confounded by what he does today. They are no longer up to date. Fact is, they may even *like* the new action of today and forget all about yesterday.

4. *Call in an Expert.*

The boss must show he is a right-now man; he wants the very best and the very latest for his library. He must show he is impartial. If what the boss wants is radical, he can leave it all up to an outside expert. The outsider will have no axe to grind; he will be objective. And the boss can prove he is really modest; he can show he knows he does not know everything. So he calls in an expert.

Who says the expert is an expert? The boss says it, who else? The boss says it loudly, he says it firmly, he says it often. That is the stuff experts are made of. Naturally, before the boss says anything, he will make sure that the expert will tell him to do what he wants to do. He will find out what the guy has done for other bosses who called him an expert.

So the boss will call in his expert. He will have the expert write a big report and he will have the report published with the blare of trumpets and with the expert's name on the cover. Then the boss will go bravely ahead and do his radical thing he wanted to do. And if anyone so much as squeaks, the boss can shrug his shoulders and say "But the expert said . . ." (Even better, after the expert has departed he may call in your boss as an expert in *his* library some day. What is good for your library is good for the boss. Or is that the way you say it?)

5. *There are Two Reasons.*

For every act of an administrator there are two reasons: 1) The Public Reason, and 2) The Real Reason. If the boss works hard at it, he can, no doubt, cook up an extra Public Reason, just in case of need. It is all only logic. There *must* be a reason; else why would a smart man like your boss have done it?

And that is why your boss bugs you. He has to follow his Five Laws (First Round). What about you? You follow the Five Laws (Second Round), that's what you do. Remember?

Five Laws of Library Administration (Second Round)

1. *Don't Rock the Boat.*

Every day in every way your library gets better and better. That's right, friend, accent the positive. Keep the faith, baby. Don't be a gloom and doomer. Don't ask questions. You don't want the patrons or your colleagues to have doubts, do you? Destroy their faith in Santa Claus? Of course not, Virginia. That new boss is the best little old thing that ever happened to your library. Remember how awful it used to be with the old boss? Backward and backward every day.

2. *Help the Boss Rock.*

Sure, library circulation went down after he came. Is that bad? Of course, it is not bad. Circulation went down because the boss did his job so well. He sold everybody on books. He got everybody to borrow books. He talked everybody into reading the book he borrowed. If the borrower could not read, the boss got him to learn to read. And everybody became literate. And then everybody could get a job, and everybody earned so much money he could buy his own books. He had to spend the money somehow. That's all there is to it. What's wrong about low circulation?

So now the boss can use book money to increase your salary? But you forget: Emphasize the positive. You already have a big salary; remember? How can the boss spend all that money? It's up to you to think up ideas and tell him.

3. *Help the Boss Keep Rocking.*

So the one-time borrowers now have their own books. Tell the boss to get something they don't have; that will bring them back to borrow again. The boss can buy a swimming pool and lend it to them. He can get a golf course and lend it to them. The library is a materials center, isn't it? What is more material than a golf course?

But the library is more than just a materials center; it is an *instructional* materials center. So your boss can buy a swimming pool, and the ex-book-borrowers can borrow the pool and you can instruct them in how to use it. They will flock to borrow the golf course and you will instruct them how to use it. Remember Course 777 in good old graduate library school: Fun and Games? (Only the graduate school dean was a fuddy duddy and they had to call good old 777 "Instructional Materials Center Instruction" to get it past Eagle Eye's office.)

Like I say, accent the positive. Help the boss keep on rocking. Feed the patrons instruction till it runs out of their ears. Lend them paste and brush and instruct them how to use it and make them a one toothpaste family again. Lend them the Long Brand and instruct them in the mystery of how to keep the burning end out of the beard of the man they talk to. So the ex-borrowers want to win the bridge tournament? So they want to solve the cross word puzzle?

Don't complain. Accent the positive. Give them the next hand at bridge. Give them the cross word. But give it with a smile.

The Massage is the message, baby.

4. *Don't Damn the Expert.*

He will be a nuisance. He will ask you a lot of foolish questions. He will hold a stop watch while you go to the powder room. Sure he will. He will even put you in a little box on a chart, and he will draw a line to another little box for the powder room.

But don't complain. You are not an old fogey, are you? You do want to go to the powder room in the most efficient way, don't you? You do want folks to think the boss is right, don't you?

Just remember Vergil: Forsan et haec olim meminisse iuvabit—someday you will get the last laugh. Someday that expert will finish his charts and tables and things and take his stop watch and his cash and go on his way rejoicing. And he will leave you to carry out the changes he says the library should make. And then you will carry them out. Yes, indeed. You will carry them out, all right—but that snoopy guy will not be there to see where you carry them.

5. *Don't Find the Flaws in the Public Reason.*

You can, of course. It is easy to find them. But don't let the boss know. The boss thinks he is a brain; don't spoil his dream. He will begin to look at you in a strange way. He may do more. And he will give you another public reason for the more he does. So believe the public reason you already have. You can catch more flies with honey than with vinegar. Who wants to catch a fly? Why you do, that's who.

So keep the faith, baby.

How to Build a Log

A good school, so it was said long ago, we are told, is a good teacher at one end of a log and a (presumably good) student at the other end. That was yesterday; in the today world we build the log with care.

When we come to build a library school building we find that here, as in every part of library work, there are Five Laws. They are brief and obvious.

1. *Let the Dean Do It.*

The Dean knows better than his Faculty what they will need and where. After all, the Faculty's notions of what is necessary will be colored by the narrow and limited experience of each within his own narrow and limited experience. The Dean can bring to the problem the broad vision of the seer who sees the problem clearly and sees it whole.

There is a corollary to this Rule: Let the Faculty think they help do it. Better yet, let the Faculty elect a Faculty Building Committee. Let the Faculty Building Committee meet with the Dean and suggest ideas and talk them out. This will give the Committee members a sense of Participating in The Decision-Making Process and if things later go wrong, the Faculty can blame the Committee no less than the Dean. Indeed, the Faculty may blame the Committee even more than the Dean; after all, the Committee members are their peers. Meanwhile the Dean can go ahead with planning the building and he can find practical reasons why this or that wish of the Committee is impractical and he can change the decisions to meet the changed conditions and he can report these actions forced upon him at the next Building Committee meeting. The Faculty and the members of the Faculty Building Committee will be, of course, really busy people; they cannot afford to waste too much time on discussion of detail; so the Committee meetings will have to be short and the Faculty will be content if now and then the Dean flits into each Faculty member's office and flips the blueprints under the Faculty member's eye and on top of what the Faculty member is working on. The Faculty member's mind will dwell on what he has beneath the blueprint as the Dean's finger moves quickly from this to that magnificent advantage and the Faculty member's mouth will probably murmur assent so that he can get back at the stuff under the blueprint as soon as possible.

There is a second corollary to this Rule: Don't forget the Architect. He also will have ideas about how the building can go. He will be able to show the Dean how this idea of the Faculty Building Committee (he does not like) fails to leave the necessary two inches at the building line or at least violates the zoning ordinance. This leaves the Dean free to decide himself how the thing should go; after all, one cannot take the valuable time of the Faculty to decide every piddling detail. What else is a Dean for if not to save the time of the Faculty?

Finally, there is a third corollary to this Rule: Don't forget the Cash. If the Dean does not like some idea of the Faculty or the Faculty Committee, let him look to the cash. Probably the idea will cost too much and he will have to drop it—regretfully.

2. *It's what's out front that counts.*

Or, to put it in more poetic terms: Build thee more stately mansions. Or, again to quote someone or other: Beauty is its own excuse for being.

This means broad green lawns, tall stately doors, at least one tower, broad shiny halls with big stretches of window. Above all, it means that the Executive Suite will be the most impressive part of the building. There will be an Outer Office and Inner Offices and (well hidden from the gaze of the curious and the ignoble strife of the madding crowd) the carpeted hideaway for the Dean where he can think Big Thoughts and make Big Plans without hindrance.

3. *Little Things for Little Things.*

This is a general law, but it will apply first of all to Faculty offices. If the halls and lawn and Executive Suite are generous and sweeping it is only common sense that there will be little room and little cash left for Faculty offices. They can be cubby holes with tiny, tinny desks, cheap, modernistic looking chairs, cheap wooden shelving and little bulletin boards where the Faculty may hang their mementos without spoiling the handsome walls with nails to hang stuff on. Winter and stormy weather will require a place for outer clothing, but individual closets will be an obvious waste of cash and space; better have some hooks on the wall for coats and hats. These will be ugly but remember Law 2: It's what's out front that counts. Obviously a Faculty office is not out front.

4. *Beware the Book, but Gather the Gadgets.*

Put no library in the library school building. After all, there is the university library downstairs or next door or somewhere. What better training for the library school student than to have to use a real library under real library conditions? This will, of course, flood the library reference rooms with library school students working on the artificial problems posed in their reference courses. It will crowd the catalog with students working on the artificial problems posed by their cataloging classes. It will flood the reserve book room with library school students doing the required reading for all their courses. But does not the library exist to serve the university students and are not library school students university students? Moreover, this is a today school. And everyone knows today is not a book world. Today is a non-book world.

So the Building will gather the gadgets. All things audio-visual will jam its every corner. Every class room will be geared for audio-visual production and presentation.

5. *Standardize.*

Let each class room duplicate every other class room, each faculty office every other faculty office, let each part of the building have the same temperature in winter and in summer. It will be more efficient, it will cost less to build it this way, and it will avoid faculty jealousies. Standardization will, of course, bring monotony. The long hall flanked by duplicate offices could pass as a hospital's long hall flanked by bedrooms; but only until the visitor looks for the beds in the rooms.

And that, dear reader, is how to build a library school building. Simple enough if you just follow the simple Five Laws.

If You Input the Output Where Does the Putout Go?

"Our students are our input and our alumni are our output." Miss Krasby adjusted her glasses and cleared her throat and looked solemnly around the table. "Even with a distinguished faculty the output will be poor if the input is poor."

"You mean it all depends on the hog, not the little old sausage grinder?" Professor Gaggle was not fond of jargon. Miss Krasby ignored him.

"What this school must seriously consider is how to set its admission standards with the objective of maximizing the quality of the input to the point where we minimize the poor quality of the output."

"You have a splendid idea there, Miss Krasby." The Dean nodded sagely. The Dean liked to nod sagely to faculty; it makes faculty think the Dean thinks highly of what faculty has just said, and Deans get along better with faculty who think their Deans think highly of what they say. He smiled. "Just what did you have in mind to achieve this objective?" The Dean knew well what Miss Krasby had in mind (she had taken an hour yesterday to tell him); he also knew well she would like to get it out of her mind again.

"What we need, Mr. Dean, is a feedback from the input before we allow it to become input. If we have feedback then we can know if the candidates for admission will be good input. Then, if the faculty is not remiss in its teaching function, we shall significantly maximize the quality of our output."

"Hear, hear," murmured Professor Gaggle. "The only problem now remaining is how we get the input to putout the feedback before we put the input in. What are your ideas, madam, on that question?" Professor Gaggle tried to look sage but it was no go.

The Dean gulped; he could not look sage either now. But he had to say something at once. "Yes, Miss Krasby, how do we do it?" He managed a weak smile.

Miss Krasby, unlike the Dean, was not at a loss for words. "The answer is obvious: our alumni. We must put on a crash program to get feedback from our alumni on what they think should be the qualities most to be desired in our output. Then this feedback will be input to an alumni program of recruitment. The output of the alumni program will be input of maximized quality for the school; and that in turn will eventuate in maximized quality in output."

Professor Gaggle smiled sweetly. "Amazing! A circle of perpetual motion. Round and round it goes and each time round is better than the time before. I repeat it: Amazing!"

The Dean tried to think of something; he could only frown. Miss Krasby gulped. Professor Gaggle kept on smiling, and then he kept on talking.

"The only trouble with my learned colleague's splendid idea is this: If our present output's quality is now minimal instead of maximal, then how can we look to our present output to putout feedback which can be utilized to maximize the quality of future input?" Professor Gaggle smiled modestly about at the faculty. This jargon business was not so bad after all once you got the hang of it.

Miss Krasby plunged in: "Some people look only at what

seems to be the hard side of things." When she wished she could use short words. "Of course, we'd have to be careful about whom we chose from the alumni to depend on and careful about which of their ideas we adopted before we could go ahead with the program."

Professor Gaggle's smile became a grin. "But, Professor Krasby, that would be to fall back on the little old sausage grinder after all if we have the faculty pick and choose among the alumni and then pick and choose among their ideas—stir up the output till we found what we wanted."

Professor Krasby could only nod. Gaggle frowned and went on.

"There is one little thing that bothers me. Your plan calls for feedback from the alumni on what they think should be the qualities most to be desired in our output. I believe that was what you said, was it not, give or take an output or two?"

Miss Krasby nodded glumly. What was the old coot about? Professor Gaggle only smiled and went on.

"But wouldn't this mean simply to fall back on what practicing librarians—and that's what our alumni are—want the school to produce? Should the school follow the profession—give the libraries what they think they want? Or should the school lead the profession?"

Miss Krasby gulped again. Only last faculty meeting she had delivered her usual fifteen minute lecture on this point.

The Dean rushed in with oil for the troubled water. "Of course, the school should lead the profession. Miss Krasby made that quite clear last time and the whole faculty endorsed the idea."

Professor Gaggle bowed to his Dean and smiled again.

Just Medium Media

She was a good looking young woman and she looked good in miniskirts. Having noted the essentials, J. Parkington Poot settled back to listen to what she was saying.

Miss Minerva Veenis was doing her thing: talking up instructional media centers to the rest of the elementary school faculty during the Wednesday Noon Discussion Hour. Parky took a dim view of IMC, but it was remarkable how Minnie improved the view. Parky listened intently. Parky's faculty listened politely.

The topic of the day was a government sponsored study of nine media centers established in three ghetto areas since 1965. Minnie began by reading aloud the report of interviews in one school; it seemed typical of all the reports. After each point she paused for comment; Parky liked audience participation in these faculty discussions.

"All the interviewed pupils enjoyed going to the media center most of the time for a variety of reasons."

"Did they really enjoy it, or did they just say they enjoyed it because they thought the interviewer wanted that answer?" Miss Matilda Griswold was too old for miniskirts, Parky noticed.

Miss Veenis smiled patiently. "Good question, Matty, but that is a problem with every study based on interviews, isn't it? We just have to remember that it is there and make allowances."

"Did they enjoy it enough to go back when they were not scheduled to go?" Matty was a persistent female, thought Miss Veenis. But she turned on another smile.

"Frankly, they did not go except when they were scheduled to go, but the study did not go into that . . ."

"That's strange," purred Miss Griswold. "Very strange if the study insisted that the kids liked to go."

"Suppose you go on to the reasons the children gave for liking the Center, Miss Veenis." Parky was really with Matty Griswold, but time was running short.

Miss Veenis smiled warmly at Parky and began with the first reason:

"Twelve liked to read."

"You mean they have books in instructional media centers?" Sol Suckerman tried to sound incredulous and someone snickered. Minnie blandly went on to the next reason:

"Nine thought the librarian was nice."

Everyone laughed and Parky thought Miss Veenis looked nice. Smoothly Minnie read the next reason:

"Eight liked someone to read to them."

Parky liked for Miss Veenis to read to him. He was amazed to hear himself speak out: "Just like the kids used to be in the school library."

Miss Veenis gulped. What was wrong with old Parky Poo? She flashed a bright smile at Parky: "But, sir, the instructional media center does not displace the school library. It simply expands the school library to include much more than books." She thought her logic silenced Parky; actually it was her smile that made him look sheepish.

Minnie moved triumphantly to the next reason:

"Seven enjoyed the film strips." She beamed at Parky. "There was no film strip in the school library, sir."

"Why did the little monsters like the film strips? Because

it's easier to look at pictures than to read?" Sol Suckerman had returned to the fray.

Miss Veenis smiled tolerantly. "Of course, it's easier to look at a film than to read! But just because a thing is easier does not make it wrong, does it? What a Puritan you turn out to be, Sol!" Everybody grinned. Sol Suckerman a Puritan!

Sol was not to be put aside so lightly. "But, Minnie, everybody says Johnny can't read and you know it. Maybe too much film in school *is* why."

"Well . . ." There was a loud silence. Then Parky came to the rescue.

"Your question, Mr. Suckerman, hangs on another question: How does Johnny learn to read? By being taught well or by practicing reading? It may be that the teaching is at fault. I suspect that it is more efficient for Johnny to learn by film instead of by reading when he can." Parky was not convinced himself, but time was running short. Minnie smiled gratefully at him.

She read the next reason:

"Six found the media center pretty."

Parky thought any place would be pretty with Miss Veenis in it. But again in amazement he heard his own voice: "The children thought our school library was pretty too."

Miss Veenis turned red. She must be patient with the old geek. Where did they get principals anyway? "But, sir, just as I was saying a while ago, the instructional media center does not replace the school library. It only expands it."

Parky wondered vaguely why he had fallen into the trap again, and Miss Veenis turned back to her paper:

"Five relished the quiet of the media center."

Parky remembered that some kids had liked the quiet in the school library, but he said nothing. Miss Griswold had another angle: "I read in some library journal the other day—heaven only knows why I looked into it!—anyway, I read that it is the in-thing to stop this silence in libraries."

Minnie smiled sweetly. "I'm glad when faculty look into library journals even if they don't know why. Yes, Matty, you are right. I saw that article too. I guess it just means that five kids in this study like things the way they are." She took up the next reason:

"Four liked to look at pictures."

Sol Suckerman grunted: "Pictures!" Everyone smiled again and Miss Veenis read on:

"One liked to listen to records."

Sol exploded: "The spoken word and the pictured word! No wonder Johnny can't read!"

Parky had been making notes on a pad of paper. "Miss Veenis, these are some rather interesting statistics. Twelve students like the instructional media center because they like to read. Seven like filmstrips, four like to look at pictures, and one likes to listen to records; that makes a total of twelve who like the audio-visual part of the center. All the rest of them like things they could find in the school library: A nice librarian, being read to, a pretty room, a quiet room."

"Well, sir, I suppose that means we shall just have to strengthen our audio-visual collection and promote its use."

"But does that follow? Is there any hard evidence that children do always learn more and better from audi-visual media than from the old-fashioned book? Is there any hard evidence that Sol is not right about why Johnny can't read?"

Miss Veenis glared. The faculty smiled discreetly. The bell rang. Time for class. The faculty rushed out. Parky sat and stared at the blackboard. Was he getting too old for this job?

Little Man in a Big Way

The little man in the bright plaid suit ran up the broad stairs and banged the huge knocker on the bronze gate. Slowly the gate squeaked open. Inside stood a skinny young man with long black hair and a long black beard.

"Yes?" The young man's voice rang clear as a bell.

The little man outside stepped back. A hippie? This was too much! Down there he had always managed a smile and he had always managed to get along with them. But a hippie here? He would have to speak to the manager. But first he would have to get inside. He smiled his famous smile and issued his pronouncement: "J. Kankerton Perly III, Director of Gassington Public Library. I believe I have a reservation."

The young man smiled brightly and he threw the door wide. "Your reservation is being processed now. Please come in and have a seat." Perly strode inside and dropped into a deep cushioned chair. The young man perched on his desk and stared at Perly with wide black eyes.

"You know, sir, I thought your reservation statement was fascinating."

Perly smiled, this time without effort. "I am glad to hear that."

"Yes, you see, sir, you have done so much. I am not a librarian myself, and your story stirred my curiosity. While

we wait, I hope you won't mind if I ask you about some
things you said."

Perly's smile broke into a grin. Very charming young
man, after all. He would have to compliment the manager
on his choice of a receptionist. "By all means, young man.
Please ask anything you wish."

"Well, sir, for a beginner, what is a library? I often
passed the big building in my home town; but, you know,
I never went inside."

Perly's smile faded. A hard core job here after all. "Well,
a library is . . ." Perly's voice faded into nothing for a moment. What, indeed, *is* a library? Vaguely he remembered
some words out of library school long ago. "A library is a
collection of books and non-book material organized for
use." Perly frowned. Why did it sound so formal?

The young man also turned serious. "Use by whom, sir?"

"Use by the public." This was easy; Perly became confident again. "The library is tax-supported; it belongs to the
public." He must remember the phrase; it would be good
to open a speech sometime.

The young man's face lighted up. "Ah, yes. I remember
now. You said it in your reservation statement. You serve
the public. It must be a wonderful thing, sir, to serve the
public with books. To get everybody to read the very best
there is. To have the reading room crowded day and night.
To have people borrowing books right and left. To bring
light where there has been darkness. It must make you feel
all warm inside just to think about it."

Perly did feel all warm inside. A fine young man. The
young man went on.

"I especially liked that part about the ghetto. Where you
said you did not sit and wait for poor people to come into
your library; you went out into the street to get them. You
had young women telling stories to poor boys and girls on
every street corner, and you had rock and roll dancing in

the street every night. You were really with it, sir. Gassington has been lucky to have you all these years."

Perly beamed. "Well, maybe that's putting it a bit strongly."

"Oh, I am sure you are only being too modest, sir. But I did wonder about one thing. Are you sure it was more important for poor people to have stories and dancing than decent food and decent places to live?"

Perly gulped. So! A young smarty after all. "Well, you see, it really would not have helped build many houses or feed many people if the library budget had gone for that. Anyway, the story-telling and the dancing helped take people's minds off their troubles. The Mayor even gave me a Good Citizens' Award for my contribution towards keeping the city cool when other towns were having riots."

"Yes I noticed in your statement." The young man's voice was dry. "Well, anyway, sir, I liked the business-like way you ran the library. Not every library, I am sure, has the luck to have a director who brings in a consultant to make a systems analysis and then takes action. Why, you saved six and a half cents on every book cataloged and one-half cent on every book loaned."

Perly smiled warily. Where was this going now? The young man also smiled but not warily.

"What did you do with all the money you saved? Get more books? Increase service to the ghetto? Your statement did not say."

"Why—we reduced the library budget. The Mayor and the Council were most appreciative . . ."

"I am sure they were. But, sir, a while ago you said that a library is for use by the public. That would seem to mean that when you save the public's money you should invest the saving in service to the public, wouldn't it? Surely the library exists not to save money or to make money but to spend money. Wouldn't you agree, sir?" The young man's black eyes stared innocently at Perly.

But Perly scuttled on to something else. "Every year we had a splendid National Library Week. Big publicity, pretty girls, a hot shot band, big parades, all sorts of excitement and involvement. People crowded into the library. People who had—lots of them—never been there before."

The young man nodded. "Yes, I am sure it must have been mighty exciting for everyone. I believe you mentioned that the NLA gave an award for that. But tell me more about it. Did the crowds keep on coming back after the Week was over? Did they get good books? Did they learn to read and find helpful information?"

Perly frowned. "Well, there was some letting up afterward. You can't keep people steamed up all the time you know."

The young man clucked sympathetically. "Yes, I guess you're right. Anyway, it would have sent library expenses up if they had kept coming back."

Perly rushed on. "I built a magnificent new building. That Carnegie monstrosity had seen its day long ago. There's lots of good modern equipment in the new building too."

"Yes I noticed that, sir. Gassington was sure lucky, all right, I guess. Only one thing bothered me. Did you really need a new library building more than they needed new houses in the ghetto? Could you have got by with just face lifting your old building? And how many houses in the ghetto would the new building have paid for?"

Perly squirmed. Then he swallowed his anger and once more managed a shadow of his famous smile. "Do you suppose my reservation is processed by now?"

"Oh, I am sorry, sir. I was so wrapped up in what you were telling me about libraries that I forgot to tell you. Yes, the reservation is processed, sir."

Perly was puzzled. He had seen no messenger bring the papers. He had heard no phone—why, there was no phone on the young man's desk.

The young man smiled once more. "I am the processor, sir. We don't have centralized processing here yet; we're a bit old fashioned, I suppose. But that's all right, sir. Everything is in order, sir."

Slowly J. Kankerton Perly III, Director of Gassington Public Library, sank into the floor—perky little man; bright, plaid suit; deep cushioned chair—everything.

Look to the Closet, Friend

O Mum, dear Mum, Daddy's hung you in the closet and we're feeling so glum.

Daddy (they say) was once young and debonair. That was when the Reverend Melvil Dewey married the Hired Girl in the Ancient House of Reading to the Heir of the House, our Daddy.

It was love at first sight and it worked. Mum knew how to make the House go, a regular Little Orphan Annie who washed the cups and saucers up and swept the crumbs away.

And they lived happily ever after for a while. Mum swept and brushed and the House was so clean and every piece of furniture was in its place even after we children began to come. There was always food on the table, nothing fancy, of course, but good, wholesome food.

We were the children of that happy couple and we rejoiced and were exceeding glad and we took in the wisdom of Mum with our milk. And we shared the wisdom of Mum with all the Heathen who knew not Reading. And we taught these Heathen to share the Wisdom of Mum with other Heathen who knew not Reading. And life was good.

And yet, as time marched on, Daddy got restless. Surely there was something more to life than Reading in a clean house with furniture you could always find in its place. Indeed, did you need all this claptrap just to be a Reading? Need he always follow the ancient ways of his Ancient

House? Had the Hired Girl tricked him into the Wrong Life?

Daddy went to see a marriage counsellor named Williamson, and after he came away life was never again the same. The good Dr. Williamson told Daddy that he was right, that what he needed was a Change; somehow he had to get away from Mum.

So Daddy came home and began to sneer at Mum and ask what else she could do besides keep house and have children who kept house and went around playing house with other children. He forgot that we were *his* children also.

Then Daddy began to step out with Other Dames of Younger Vintage. Some were younger than us, his children. Daddy liked them. They agreed with him. They said he was indeed cut out for nobler things in this life. Daddy walked on clouds.

First came University. She thought the good Dr. Williamson was right, of course. She told Daddy he needed only sit and think noble thoughts. Why bother to clean the house and arrange the furniture? Much better first debate and decide how best to do these tedious things in the Ideal House. Once he had found the Plan, asked Daddy, who would do the dirty work? Why, people born to do dirty work, of course. Not Daddy. This pleased Daddy.

So Daddy hung Mum in the closet and the Reverend Dr. Williamson married Daddy to University. And University swore that the great House of Reading should suffer wrong no more.

Then came Documentation. She frowned and scoffed at what Mum had done, and she told Daddy he needed only one thing: Debate and decide how best to wash the cups and saucers up and sweep the crumbs away. No point in going to all that trouble unless he had a Plan, was there now? Daddy agreed. But who *would* do the work, once he had found the Plan? Well . . . She had a sister.

Then came Information Science (Daddy never did know if there was one or more of her). Why bother, she said sweetly, with all this traditional housewifely drudgery? Daddy agreed. Why indeed? First debate and decide how best to clean the house and arrange the furniture. Who would do the work once he found the Plan? Well . . . She had a sister.

So last of all came Automation. She swept us all off our feet. Life could now be real dreamy again. Like the others, she sneered at Mum and her tiresome way of life. Why bother with it? Why do the cups and saucers at all? Why brush the crumbs at all? Unlike the others, she brought an answer: Just dump your little problems into her handy little machine and lo—they were good as gone. Life *was* dreamy again.

But then Automation began to look at Daddy and his children. Why bother with his Reading House? True, it was an Ancient House. But it was also an old-fashioned house. Who wants to read anyway? Just ask her handy little machine; it will answer your every question. If you do insist on having a book in your grubby hand, there is always the drug store and its paperbacks or the machine and its printouts. So why bother with the House? Except, of course, the closet; you can always use a closet.

O Dad, dear Dad, the New Dame's hung you in the closet and we're feeling so bad. But really bad. We mean it.

We're hanging there with you.

Macrothought in Miniskirt

The Wise Man from the East was slender and white haired and frail, but he spoke with the authority of the seer.

"I think he's cute." Sue's voice rang out over the hall; she had forgotten the microphone at her side. Sam blushed as people laughed and turned to look. Even the Wise Man was smiling gently as he walked out leaning ever so slightly on the cane. It had been a good session; people had listened; they believed. He could now go and rest and leave discussion to his disciple.

The disciple, a fussy little man with a British accent, took his stand behind the podium. "Questions or comments?"

Sam rose. "Sir, we have heard a lot today about the facet. But is anything new about the facet except its name? Didn't Dewey use facets?"

The fussy little man smiled patiently. This was an easy one. "Dewey did use facets, of course. But he didn't know it and he didn't have a scientific way of using them."

Sue pulled at Sam's coat, but he blazed away: "What, I ask you, is the basic difference between 822.33 and O11,2,J64? Each is the result of facets and a facet formula. Dewey's string of symbols means Literature—English—Drama—Elizabethan—Shakespeare. Colon's string means Literature—Modern English—Drama—Shakespeare. The only difference is that Dewey's symbols are all in one place in his scheme where you can easily find them while each Colon symbol is in a separate table where you have to dig it out before you can put it with the others."

The little man almost sneered. "The difference, young man, is the difference between accident and design. You picked a place where your notion worked. But just listen to Dewey himself." Triumphantly he fished out the xerox sheet; he had hoarded it for just such a moment. He read Dewey's words in a high squeaky voice:

"Detaild explanation of selection and arranjement of the many thousand heds wud be tedius; but everywhere filosophic theory and accuracy hav yielded to practical usefulness . . . The skeme givs us for each topic as it wer, a case of 9 pijeonholes, with a larj space at the top; and we uze them as every practical business man uses such pijeonholes about his desk. If . . . there ar less than 9 main topics, it is often convenient to uze the extra spaces for subdivisions."

The little man beamed. "There, young man, what do you make of that? Dewey did *use* facets. But he didn't really know a facet from a hole in a desk." He snickered.

Sue jerked at Sam's coat again. "See? Sit down, Sam, please sit down."

Sam was in no mood for sitting. "So what? Practical usefulness was all Dewey wanted—not a lot of philosophy. He said it himself in what you just read. What matter if he did ignore facets now and then so long as his scheme helped people find books? What more could you reasonably ask?"

The little man dragged out all his patience. "I would ask that a classification be an intellectually respectable system, not a hodgepodge of made-up numbers. There are already more things in this world than you and I can dream of, my young friend. Haven't you heard of the explosion of knowledge? The Colon system gives us the material to work out a place for each bit of new knowledge as it comes along."

Sam was not convinced. "And meanwhile Colon would make each little classifier in even the tiniest library dig out a batch of symbols from hither and yon and string them together for each book on each of the everyday things of life we already know about, just so some big shot classifier in some big shot research library can build a number in case a book comes along on something nobody knows of now."

The little man drew to his full height. "That my dear sir, is a pretty simplistic way of washing down the drain a whole philosophical and systematic approach to all knowledge now and yet to be—"

"Oh, come off it, sir. The Master himself makes no such claim. Colon in its present shape is for books and books only—Macrothought, not microthought."

The little man gasped. "But surely you don't know what you say, young man. Of course, the present Colon is only for Macrothought but it sets the stage for organizing Microthought. And what a magnificent stage it is! Five Fundamental Categories—"

"Hold it, hold it!" Sam could have none of this. "How do you *know* there are *exactly* five fundamental categories, no more, no less? How do you know their sequence is the magic PMEST? Revelation perhaps? Reason perhaps now and then? But proof—really, honest proof? Never."

"Well . . ." This was a new one for the little man. He had come up against tough unbelievers before. But this! He switched to attack. "Well, young man, at least Colon is not a heaped up, cooked over scheme like Dewey—and anyway, what's so wonderful about Dewey? Practical usefulness he said; practical usefulness *you* say. But what is your *proof* that it is practically useful—?"

"Only proof I can think of is that Dewey has lasted almost a century and is used in most American libraries. Somebody must think it works."

Everyone laughed. Sue stopped pulling at Sam's coat.

The little man rallied to the attack again. "Well, at least you will have to admit that Colon is intellectually respectable."

"Intellectually respectable?" Sam smiled sweetly. "Is it now? Or is it only an appeal to our snobbery? Fundamental Categories, Rounds of Manifestation, Levels of Manifestation, Octave Device—jargon this, jargon that. Is it intellectually respectable? Or is it only an attempt to make a puzzle out of something quite simple so that ordinary people will gape and think there is magic and mystery in this tired old business we call library service?"

"Anyone else have a question?" The little man was wistful.

Sam yielded to Sue's tug at his coat; he sat down.

Two jargon-hours later the crowd drifted out onto the street. Sue bubbled. "What a wise and wonderful old man! It makes you feel warm and good all over just to hear him talk!"

Sam raged. "Wise old man, she says. Wonderful old man, she says. Five laws of library science and fifty books of library science while in his homeland millions starve with never a glimpse of a book or even a facet. Why didn't he stay home and help lead his people into today? Instead he tramps out to lead the rest of the world into tomorrow—"

Suddenly Sam stood still. "Sue, do you think he really means it? Or is it all a giant hoax? So many bright men and women all over the world so enamored of his ideas—not because they understand the ideas but because of the mysterious language which hides the ideas. The Wise Man's words only *sound* English. What the words say is Eastern—strange, beautiful, elusive. Has the great man spent his life making fun of us? When we try to read his books, when we sit with open mouths as he talks, when the English disciple tries to explain it all—does he only mock us? Has he won a savage revenge for the Western intellectual imperialism inflicted on his country?"

Sue squeezed Sam's arm. "Sam, you are wonderful when you are like this. But I still think he's cute."

Model Remodelled

Fitzroy Cutterby tapped on the door and got the usual hearty "Come in!" Buddington Jones always boomed out a booming, friendly voice to prove to all his staff that he was just a booming, friendly fellow they could always count on for a booming, friendly chat about almost anything big or little that might be bothering them.

Cutterby gently opened the door to be greeted by a booming "Howdy, Fizz!" Secretly Cutterby loathed the boss's passion for nicknames, but he swallowed his distaste: "Mighty fine, Bud, mighty fine!" Secretly Jones loathed this "Bud" stuff, but it was good for staff morale. Made him just one of the boys.

Cutterby managed what he hoped was a hearty grin: "What's up, Bud?"

Jones managed an answering smile. He tapped the open copy of *Library News* on his desk. "Remember that fellow, Boomsby, who came around a year ago to interview you and Scarsby? Working on a doctoral study of what he called 'middle management.' "

Cutterby nodded without a smile. He did, indeed, remember. A brash, snoopy young man with no library experience to speak of who took up more than an hour with questions about Cutterby's job; he had been patient with the fellow only because Jones wanted him to.

"Seems he's finished his study and got his degree and

here he's published a summary of it. He says there are three kinds of middle managers. He calls them Models. Specialist, Executive, and Technocrat. Fizz, you're a Technocrat all right. Anyway you're in charge of technical services. But you're not like what he says you should be. What's wrong? What did you tell him? Why didn't he use it?"

Jones put on the face of the friendly, concerned administrator.

Cutterby only stared. "What does he say?"

"Well, for one thing, Fizz, you are always wanting me to dig up money to send you to NLA or some other professional meeting. Boomsby says you are a member of NLA, but not active professionally. Why can't you be like Boomsby says? I'm glad you joined NLA. But it costs money to send you to meetings, you know; and it takes you away from the job. Why can't you be like Boomsby says you should be?"

"But, Bud, Boomsby was not going to say what we should be. He said he only wanted to know what we are."

"Should be, are—so what?" Jones grabbed his fleeting patience and put back on his patient smile. "It does really take quite a bit of money, you know; just think what it would do to my budget if we sent everybody wherever he wanted to go?"

Cutterby remembered that he did not get money to go to every NLA meeting, but he also remembered not to say it.

Jones swept on: "Boomsby says you do not publish. But you *do* publish, Fizz, old boy. Just last month you had that thing in *Library Journal* on how we should employ more minority group people in libraries. You are right, of course, you know. But it takes time to write articles, and you stir things up."

"But I wrote it on my own time."

"I know," Jones smiled sincerely as if he really did know. "But you signed it as a member of this staff, and it might give people the idea that you were stating the official policy of the Library."

"But, Bud, at the last staff meeting you said exactly what I said in the article."

"We're getting off the subject," said Jones quickly. "We were talking about professional activity. Why did you spend so many hours meeting with the Catalog Code Revision Committee? Boomsby says the Technocrat is not active professionally. What's more, Boomsby says you are more concerned with technical skills than with theory. Catalog code revision is theory. Theory with a capital T. And it isn't practical. We can't afford to use the new code in this library; you surely must have known it when you were working on it."

"But, Bud, it really is a better code—even with the compromise LC made us stick in."

"Boomsby says you are inherently conservative and you resist change. Boy, he sure missed the boat there too. Why can't you be like Boomsby says? Teamwork, Fizz, teamwork is what we need to win the game."

"What game, Bud?"

But Jones was off on a new track. "Boomsby says you are interested in efficiency, production measurement, maintenance of routines. But you are not, Fizz old boy, you are not interested at all—How much does it cost you to catalog a book?"

Cutterby smiled wearily. It was not a new question. "Bud, you know I have not the foggiest notion how much it costs to catalog a book. Every book has its own problems. Oh, I could take time out and measure this and that and divide this by that and give you some sort of exact answer; but what would it mean? What I do know is that no book comes into this library and spends more than two days before it is cataloged and on the shelf for use."

"And another thing." Jones was particularly aggrieved.

"Boomsby says you are highly satisfied with your salary and you are not very mobile. All I know is that you would have been mobile several times if I had not made your salary more satisfactory."

Cutterby grinned. "Is that all, Bud?"

Jones nodded. He glanced back at the Boomsby paper: "The Technocrat is loyal to his superiors."

National Library Day

Don't look now but behind you is a skeleton, the skeleton of a Frenchman, 300 years old dangling in an ancient cabinet, "a very convenient oblong covert of timber which opening with three doors exposes ye entire parts of him to view." Why did the Frenchman walk away and leave behind so useful a part of his anatomy? Not, I assure you, dear friends, in a flash of Celtic pique because he had lost a girl. No sir, it was grand beau geste toward the greater glory of man and his education forever.

For this was no ordinary skeleton; instead, it was one of the prize parts of an instructional materials center (known to the irreverent as an IMC), the 17th century Library of the University of Edinburgh (see *Library History*, Spring 1967, p. 23).

The skeleton shared its honors with another grand material: "a corn of a considerable bigness cut from the great toe above the nail" of an Englishman, extracted from the toe on March 3, 1692 but extracted from its owner, "Mr. James Clerk, Graver to the Mint House" only when the Librarian (or as we should call him today, the IM Centrist) William Henderson "prevailed with ye party to obtain it."

There were other materials in the Center too. Books (of course, friend, of course, if you insist on mentioning such common and unhelpful objects), maps, pictures, globes of the world, mathematical instruments, microscopes, a "writ-

ing engine"—But are these not listed in the catalog of 1703?
Go and look there, friend. But be sure to remember the
useful color coding: white on black for skeletons, purple on
red for corns and other useful colors for other useful materials.

How up to date is *your* IMC, my friend? Have you a
Frenchman in the closet; and what about the corn department? If you have such are they cataloged with colors and
all that so a feller can get at them in a hurry on his way out
to lunch just before he has to meet his class? Keep up with
the ghosts, my friend, keep up with the ghosts.

Don't look now but behind the IMC is another ghost,
Aristophanes of Byzantium, chief of Ptolemy's national library of Egypt at Alexandria. Seems there was another
national library at Pergamum and the story goes that Eumenes II of Pergamum tried to entice Aristophanes to come
to Pergamum and work for his national library. But Ptolemy
got wind of this unprofessional conduct and he snapped
into action. He slapped Aristophanes into the hoosegow
and he slapped an embargo on papyrus. Eumenes, alas, had
to make do without Aristophanes and with vellum.

National libraries and national librarians are still sometimes a problem. Two differences perhaps: 1) Aristophanes
was a scholar. 2) His government wanted to keep him so
badly it took drastic action to achieve that objective. But
maybe these are not differences after all; maybe there has
simply been no occasion to use them. Let Bulgania beware.
If they try to entice our national librarian away, we may
slap an embargo on comic books and force them to make
their own.

And behind Aristophanes (perhaps along with him)
there is another ghost. Sir Thomas Bodley writing his Librarian, Dr. Thomas James, Sept. 11, 1601: "But for the
point of your marriage, I might by no meanes yelde vnto it:
holding it absurd in yow or in any, for sundrie great re-

spectes . . ." What, dear friends, is the status of librarians today? Consider Aristophanes; consider Dr. James. March we not onward and upward? We even talk of joining a union to preserve our rights and privileges—and salaries.

And look behind James: See beaming John Langdon Sibley of the noble Harvard library confronted by his President who inquires why his Librarian is so happy. All the books are on the shelves save two—and this minute he is marching to the delinquent professor's house to retrieve them. Poor John Langdon Sibley; he had not discovered that the police can raid houses in the dead of night to retrieve wandering books. Onward and upward, boys, onward and upward.

"I feel peculiar at this dedication—Mrs. C. too." Andrew Carnegie was dedicating his Homestead Library where only 6 years earlier (1892) the Homestead Steel Works had called in three hundred Pinkerton detectives to break a strike; and in a riot strikers and spectators had been killed by gunfire. (Sidney Ditzion, *Arsenals of a Democratic Culture* (1947) 156-7). The "needs of the urban wage-earner and his children," "uplift for the underprivileged," "to extend downward the benefits of learning," "an informed populace for wider political participation," "educational facilities" as "more favorable auspices for a stable society" (Ditzion, p. 193): the ghost of these 19th century hopes still walk in our big talk of today about the plight of the cities, and service to the "unhabituated reader." But in the heat of hot summers in Newark and Detroit and elsewhere we can only join the great steel king; we too can only "feel peculiar." Books and butter—which comes first?

"The least satisfactory feature of our present library systems is the excessive proportion which the annual cost of administration bears to the whole annual expenditure for the library. This state of things should be remedied . . . by means of mechanical appliances . . . better arrangement of

book rooms and . . . contrivances of that American ingenuity which has thus far done pretty well in devising means
of escape from much greater difficulties. Women should be
employed . . . as far as possible." Thus F. B. Perkins on "How
to Make Town Libraries Successful" in the famous *Public
Libraries* . . . *1876 Report,* p. 430. And on page 490 of
the same *Report,* William F. Poole wrote of cataloging: "It
is good economy to employ, temporarily, skilled and professional cataloguers to do the work and to train an inexpe-
rienced librarian in this and other duties of his profession."

The management of library operations to save a fast buck.
Do it with mechanical appliances, arrangement of books,
great dependence on women, training of library technicians
—the spirit of '76 is with us and we march to its drums.

We march into many a great and noble dream; some of
these dreams come true. We also march into Kansas where
in 1965 the average library was a city library whose librarian
was a woman high school graduate with some college education, and she was probably helped by one full-time or
part-time assistant. The library's total annual budget was
$3000; there were 12,000 volumes; 15,000 pieces circulated
in 1965; there were 2000 registered borrowers; the library
was open 20 hours a week; and there was generally a card
catalog but it was often out of date or only partial in its
coverage (*LJ,* June 15, 1967, p. 2343).

Hallowe'en: Do we haul our ghosts out of the attic once
a year and dust them off for a parade? Do we simply watch
the Hallowe'en parade or are we part of the parade? Is
Hallowe'en the way of life for librarians?

Let's forget The Week. Let's remember The Day. Write
ALA. Write your congressman. Let's make the name
official:

October 31: National Library Day.

Nothing Like a Dame

Now is the time for every girl to come to the aid of her profession. What profession? Why, the library profession, of course. What else?

No more of this homely, old-fashioned stuff like "Explore Inner Space: Read." "Read" again and again and again. Ok, read. But read what? A physiology textbook? How else can you explore inner space? Well, you *can* watch a television commercial with a nicely circular stomach or a maze of sinus tubes—or you can become a surgeon, I reckon. But that is not reading; also it is a lot of time and trouble.

So we dream about inner space and reading; and we silverline the dream with talk and debate about Las Vegas. We shall go to Las Vegas and we shall show the doubting world that we are too he-men and she-women in spite of how we look and what we think and say. Choose sin and shine up the image.

But Las Vegas is years and years from now. Get with it, Friend. Join the now-world (as we say on the culture frontier). What National Library Week really needs is a Miss American Library World. There is nothing like a dame. Really nothing.

Of course it is now too late to talk about this year. The redcoats have come and gone and done it; just look at the *Assistant Librarian*, December 1966 (page 233 if you are a real picky pedant).

With usual British modesty they called her "Miss Library World"—not something braggy like "Miss English Library World." (The same modesty pops out at you in other names such as "The Library Association.") They even had a "Grand Miss Library Ball."

While we dreamed of inner space and Las Vegas we lost the first battle. We cannot lose the war. Think what is at stake: Leadership in the bookly salvation of man. Surely we cannot let the British do it again.

There is always another year. Plan now for next year. Plan now for Miss Library Universe. (Note, I pray you, that we can be as modest as the British; no mention there of "American.")

We shall have a truly Grand and Equisite Miss Library Universe Ball. Flashy flowers and noisy bands and games and parades and mini skirts and swim suits and the Atlantic City Auditorium and throngs and throngs and throngs from all over the universe and songs by Bert Parks as the girl of our dreams, Miss Library Universe of the year, sweeps majestically above the heads of her court, the open-mouthed library-goers of the universe.

Explore Inner Space, indeed! It's what's up front that counts—or at least what's outside. Beauty is skin-deep. Why sure it is; at least that is beauty you can see. And there, friend, is the real "space" to explore.

We shall have full publicity. *Library Journal* will have a new cover girl every two weeks; how else can there be equal space to the candidates? Ranganathan will change the Second Law of the Library: "Every Reader his Book" will become "Every Reader his Girl." The ALA Directory will have a bright red cover and a bright black title: *Where the Girls Are.* And we shall have slogans: Forget Inner Space. Forget Outer Space. Join the Here and Now. Stop at the Library and Get your Girl. Books? Are you crazy, man? Why bother with a book when you can pick up a doll, a

living doll? Pick up more than one. No limitations on borrowing.

We shall stand on the curb and watch the guys stream
into the library. And we shall not worry about the dolls.
They will be inside all ready and waiting.

So the image makers will give way to the image watchers,
and all the culturally deprived will soak up culture by the
eye full and man will march on and on and up and up and
be infinitely perfected. And so at last the vision of the 19th
century will come true. But plug your years. Else the computers will strike you deaf as they try in vain to measure the
Great Leap Forward.

There is nothing like a dame. Really nothing.

One President to Another

The Dean studied the card: Nat Padpen, Pres. P.T.P.A. Then he looked up at the smilingly aggressive young man. "Glad to meet you, Mr. Padpen. But what is P.T.P.A.? If you have something to sell . . ."

"Not exactly, sir." The young man's voice was soft. "But in a way—I guess that's what it is if you look at it one way. You see, I am President of the Poll Takers Protective Association and you are President of the Library School Research Association. I think we can do business together."

The Dean was only puzzled. "What kind of business, Mr. Padpen?"

The young man smiled easily. "Just call me Nat. And what has the PTPA to do with the LSRA? You may not realize it, sir, but library school research has become big business. That's a nice little lobby you people have down in Washington and your government grants this year ran into millions; another year or so and we can talk of billions."

"I am sure you have been misinformed," said the Dean coldly. "Library school research is not a business. We are not out to make money. We want only to add to knowledge, the kind of knowledge that will help mankind. Considering the tremendous task to be done, our grant from the government this year was really disappointing. But I still do not know why you are here."

"Sure, sure," cooed Nat soothingly. "I understand all that, sir, and I should expect you to be modest about the grants. It was, indeed, a shame they turned down some of your proposals. Perhaps next year things will go better—especially if we can work out a deal with you."

"What!" The Dean was aghast. "How dare you come in here and talk about some kind of a deal. Sir, research is not some kind of graft—"

"Cool it, pop, cool it. I didn't mean to insult you. Call your racket anything you want. But get this straight. You take polls and my people take polls. You pay your poll takers next to nothing. Some of them even do it for only a lousy Ph.D. you give them. You are unfair to honest working men and women like my people. Nat Padpen is not about to take this kind of treatment lying down. Let your people join my union and get a decent wage for their work. If you don't, just see what *my* lobby will do to your grants next year. It's as simple as that, pop. What do you intend to do about it?"

The Dean shuddered. Blackmail!

"But, Mr. Padpen—"

"Just call me Nat." The young man's easy smile had returned.

"But—Nat—we don't get enough money in the grants to pay much for people to help us; many people are glad enough just to work to get more knowledge about how libraries can serve their—"

"So what, pop? *Ask* for more money. It's easy. And we'll help you get it like I said a while ago. So this research thing is not out to make money, you say. How about the professors who get the grants? The directors, I think you call them, and the principal investigators and the consultants and the what nots. Don't they get to keep a big chunk of this cash in addition to their regular wages? Isn't their share of the loot sometimes bigger than their wages—bigger by a whole lot?"

"Well, I suppose that to someone like you it may seem that the professors involved are generously rewarded. But in most cases, Mr. Pad—Nat—these are hard-working men and women who would be glad to take part in the research just for the good they may do and the knowledge they may discover—"

"Maybe that's your answer, pop! Just let the big shots work for nothing; they have the university wage to keep them going anyway. Then use the money you would pay them to pay a decent wage to your poll takers. I don't care how you work it out, just so your poll takers will join my union and get decent pay."

The Dean shuddered again. This Padpen might be able to face up to his men and women and to presidents of companies. Obviously he had never had to face up to professors. He struggled to reply.

"No, I hardly think that would be fair, Nat—to ask professors to do research for nothing." He had to add it quickly; Nat thought he was saying the union idea was unfair. "You see, Nat, they put in a lot of time on teaching classes and advising students and they often work overtime as it is."

"Maybe professors should have a union." The speculative gleam in his eye frightened the Dean and he rushed back to the plight of the poll takers.

Half an hour later the two Presidents sealed their deal with a handshake.

Put Your Mouth Where the Cash Is

"Well, that takes care of our fine police force nicely." Young Tom Proffil smiled his bright, easy smile and leaned back. He had been elected Mayor on a reform ticket to get the city out of the red and law and order into the streets, and this little increase in the police budget would help do both. "Next, we shall take up the Library." Proffil beamed; this would be easy.

A frumpy woman got up in the back of the room and announced that she was not happy. Young Proffil leaned forward with his concerned, easy smile and asked who she was and why she was not happy.

"I am Mrs. Bill Brophy. I am Chairman of the Library Board and I ask you: Why should a policeman with a year's experience get $7,800—exactly what we pay a librarian with 25 years experience in our Rebrok Memorial Library? Why, Mr. Mayor, why?"

Proffil gulped and managed an uneasy smile. "Well, you see, Mrs. Brophy, it's a matter of training—training and experience . . ."

Mrs. Brophy snorted. "Bill Batz had three months in police school and a year's experience. Mrs. Midge had a year's training; she has a Master's degree, Mr. Mayor. And she has, as I just said, 25 years experience. Training and experience, indeed!"

"But Mrs. Brophy, it's hard work being a cop—hard and dangerous—and he has to work overtime—"

"That old line again! Women can't do the work! But, you know, Mr. Mayor, some women *are* policewomen. And for overtime—the Library is open from nine till nine with no pay for overtime. Most of our librarians get less than the $6900 you're going to pay a rookie. What do you say to that, sir?"

Proffil's smile froze into a straight line. No time to be patient now. "Well, it's this way, Mrs. Brophy. We have to balance our priorities, don't we? It's law and order on the one side, reading on the other. Which is more important? How much time and peace for reading will you have without law and order?"

Mrs. Brophy was still unhappy. "Law and order! I know your motto, all right. But this is not New York City; it's a quiet country town. When did we have our last murder? When did we have our last rape? When?"

Young Tom dragged out his most patient smile and dug up his most patient voice. (It was an effort, but the problem was great.) "Of course, we have not had a murder or a rape lately. But that's because we take proper precautions. Only if we are always alert, only if we have a happy, well-paid police department shall we be sure to keep our record as a peaceful town."

A happy thought struck Proffil. "What about our Library Director? What do you want to say on this issue, Mrs. Gramps?"

Mrs. Brophy sat down with a groan. Proffil had found her Achilles' heel. Mrs. Gramps had inherited the job years ago when her husband died suddenly. Jake Gramps had been head of the party machine and the job had seemed a proper reward from a grateful community. Molly Gramps stood up and looked around slowly.

"Well, I really don't know what to say. We do need the

better salaries and we do need a good police force; both will take money and . . ." Her voice trailed off.

Proffil smiled his concerned smile: "And what, Mrs. Gramps? We should all like to hear from you on this important point."

Mrs. Gramps gasped and then grasped at a straw. "Well, I reckon you are right, Mr. Mayor, about that law and order thing. And if we are going to spend any money on the library I guess it should go into curtains and shelves for the railroad car. It could stand a coat of paint too."

Proffil beamed. "Splendid, Mrs. Gramps, splendid! I knew we could count on you. The idea of an old railroad car for a branch library building in the Whyte area was brilliant; it will serve a community which has needed library service for years, and it really won't cost much to revamp it into a cozy little place if—"

"Mr. Mayor, whatever gave you that idea?" Dizzy Dake had jumped to his feet and his deep voice blazed through his heavy black beard. "Nobody ever asked if we wanted an old junk railroad car in our part of town for a library! Why can't we have a nice new building like Whitey always has? Why do us black brothers all the time get only leftovers?"

Proffil squirmed. "Mr. Dake, Mrs. Gramps has the floor."

"So Mrs. Gramps has the floor!" growled Dizzy. "So what? Let Mrs. Gramps keep the floor. All I want is an answer. Do we get a decent library like the white cats have or do we have to spend all the money on the police for more of your law and order? How about it? Your Honor?" The sarcastic title sizzled.

Proffil tried to pull his concerned smile but it came out only a grimace. Mrs. Gramps had sat down in dismay so he could no longer fall back on the floor holder technique.

Dizzy plunged on: "It's like the lady said just now. We ain't had no riots or no murders lately. But that ain't promisin' nothin'." (In school Dizzy's best grades had been in grammar but that was before he had become a Leader in the Movement.)

"But, Mr. Dake, everyone in Whyte was glad when Mrs. Gramps came out with the railroad car idea, and everyone there has been working so hard to make the car into a pleasant—"

"Everyone! Who's everyone?" Dizzy burst in. "Every Tom out there, that's who. None of the black brothers. And, of course, that little white chick you'll put in the car when it's all fixed up so she can be comfortable—she's all for it. Get with it, Your Honor! Whyte's where we live. It's our library you're talking about. And we don't want no piece of painted up junk with Whitey sittin' in it tellin' us what to read."

"Why, Mr. Dake, I had no idea—"

"Of course, you had no idea, Your Honor. When did you last set your foot in Whyte? See it like it is, Baby; see it like it is. Well, how about it? Are you gonna get that piece of junk out of Whyte or not?"

"I'll get someone out there first thing in the morning, Mr. Dake."

"And how about a decent new library building with our own books in it and our own cats to run it?"

"Well, that"—the Mayor saw the Police Chief begin to look restive—"That will take some time, Mr. Dake. It will take money, you know . . ." His voice trailed as Mrs. Gramps' voice had trailed.

"Yeh, I know, Your Honor." Dake was sweetly polite. "Police or a library. Books or law and order. You pays your money and you takes your choice. Which will it be, Sir?"

Quest for a Mission

"This," announced the Chairman of the Library School Curriculum Committee, "is a very solemn occasion." With thumb and forefinger the Chairman explored his mustache and the Committee nodded in approval of both the occasion and the mustache. Both were new and what is new is good.

The Committee had just searched its soul and decided to ask the U.S. Government for a grant of $80,000 to take a good look at the School's curriculum. A curriculum must operate in the now-world and how can you hope to be able to say that your curriculum is in the now-world unless you get a government grant and find out that it is?

The Chairman took the next bus to Washington. He crept into the plush office and sat down across the big desk from the Government. The Government had a mustache too—and a goatee and a bald head and piercing eyes. The Chairman gushed out his Committee's Plan and the Government smiled and yawned. "But what kind of a study can you hope to do on $80,000? That would only be a start. You will need at least $160,000 and at least four years. You have not the slightest chance of getting a grant on such a modest project as you have outlined. You do want to live in the now-world you say; well, then begin with a now-subject and some now-time money. Why stick to your own little curriculum for your own little school? Why not plan

the ideal now-curriculum for the ideal now-school for the
now-everywhere?" The Chairman twisted in the soft chair.
Carefully he massaged his mustache and cheerfully he
yielded to the common sense of the Government. Why not,
indeed? Somehow he had just never thought of it that way.
He felt better about his high taxes. Money to such a wise
Government was money well spent.

The Chairman went home by plane and announced the
vision to his Committee and they all sat down to wait for
the reams of papers to be filled out and to wait for the return and final formal decision and to rejoice with exceeding
gladness when the decision came "Yes!"

The Great Crusade was on its way.

The Committee launched its job in a business-like way.
There was an Outline with points and points all in proper
sequence; the Government had said it was proper. The first
major item was Purpose and the second was Methods.
Under Purpose the first was to find out how each school
could answer its obligations as a part of its university and
at the same time serve the needs of society. And the first
entry under Methods was to consult educators, librarians,
and subject specialists from here, there, and everywhere.
Finally, because this was to be a now-study, the Committee
would consult the leaders of the Underprivileged.

Now came the first big question: How consult these consultants? By questionnaire? That would take time and some
would not answer, and they might not understand the questions anyway. Eyeball to eyeball confrontation: that was
the answer. Then you would know exactly what was said
and how they looked when they said it. But confrontation
where? Here again the answer was clear: Go yourselves to
consult the consultants. See them in their home environment; understand their consulting better. It would be a
nuisance to travel, but it was after all the Committee's
project; if sacrifice of travel was to be suffered it must be the

Committee to suffer. So the Committee took to the road and suffered.

The Educators all smacked their lips for the Committee and spoke at length for pages and pages all single-spaced, sometimes from memory and sometimes by reading, and always in Educationese. Luckily one member of the Committee had an advanced degree in Education, and he could translate what the learned men said; and another member of the Committee had been trained as a newspaper man, and he could cut down the translation to proper size. Turned into English and abstracted the Educators sang one refrain: "A library school is a graduate part of the University; therefore, the curriculum should have graduate content. It should teach the students to think, not how to arrange books or run a library."

Many of the Librarians spoke to the Committee in English, but they also talked at great length. The ex-Educator translated when necessary, and the ex-Newspaper man boiled it all down: "The University is often a State University; if it is not, it is a privately endowed university tax-exempt. The library school's duty is, therefore, to the taxpayer. Give us graduates who can find books and tell people where the comfort rooms are. These are what the taxpayers want when they come to the library."

The Subject Specialists gasped when they heard of the Committee's Mission. They had always guessed that librarians already had some sort of reason for the queer things they did and they had been content to do the best they could to help themselves on their own when they went to the library. There was no need to translate and little need to abstract what they said: "We want information and we want it yesterday when we want it. If there is any need for a library school, it is needed to teach subject specialists to find information for us on the double."

Last of all the Committee went to the Leaders of the

Underprivileged. The Leaders needed neither translator nor abstractor: "Just tell it like it is, man. Get our brothers into your school. Get our culture into what you teach. Get your students to bring our libraries to our people."

And that was the end of that. The Committee thought it over. "We have four answers," said the Youngest Member. "What is needed is a four-track curriculum." The Youngest Member had only lately heard of "tracks" and he liked the word. The Committee wrote its Report. Every library school in the country should have a four-track curriculum if it were to serve its university and its society. This would take more money, of course. But the Government liked to make grants. The Committee drew up a new Outline; if it worked fast it could get cash to change its own curriculum and to change every curriculum in the country.

The Chairman took the next plane to Washington. He marched into the plush office and sat down across the big desk from the Government. The Chairman gushed out his Committee's New Plan and the Government smiled and yawned. But it was a New Government that knew not the Old Government. The New Government had no mustache, no goatee, no bald head, no cash for Chairmen.

So the Committee kept the 160 grand and kept its old curriculum and every other school kepts its old curriculum and they all lived happily ever after.

Reading Maketh a Full Man

The long black car slid gently to the curb and the chauffeur released the smartly dressed man in the back seat. Big John strode across the street to the dingy bookmobile with its big new gay sign: "Books/Jobs." He took the two steps in one and bent his head low to get into the car.

Inside were two more big signs: "Be all you can be: Read" and "Read a Book and Get a Job." A young man was putting books on the shelves. He turned casually. "Anything I can—Why, Governor!" His mouth fell open.

Big John smiled his folksy smile and came to the point. "Your signs, son. What do they mean?"

The young man's mouth closed and opened again, this time with a torrent of words. He was an eager young man and he had a mission.

Books/Jobs was that mission. All the public libraries in the County were behind it and they had set up a special collection in each of the seven community centers scattered throughout the county. The collections were called "Books/Jobs Collections" because they each had five hundred books to help disadvantaged people get and hold jobs. The bookmobile travelled about the County and kept each collection fresh and useful.

Big John beamed. He owed his election to a ringing campaign for full employment but now he was finding it a bit rough to get full employment. The libraries! Who would ever have dreamed . . . ?

"Splendid! Splendid! Wonderful way for the County Libraries to invest their extra funds. Encourages individual initiative too."

The young man's torrent of words dried. "Well, you see, sir, it's a special project and there's really not much local money involved because the Libraries' funds are tied up in their regular ongoing expenses."

"Oh? Where do you get the money?"

"Well, the State Library and the State Bureau of Employment Services help a lot. We're mighty thankful for what the State has done."

Big John fell silent. He had wondered why the phrase "Books/Jobs" seemed vaguely familiar; now he knew why. That was the item in next year's budget he had cut in half just the other day. The young man went on.

"Of course, most of our money comes from the federal government, but they say that with a new administration we may have our funds cut. Perhaps you can use your influence in Washington for us, sir." His face lighted. "You can help us even more at the State House, sir. Maybe you can get the Legislature to give us more to make up for what Uncle Sam takes away."

Big John's folksy smile came back. "You can count on me, son," he boomed. "Anything I can do to help get jobs for the jobless I'll sure try to do. It's a big problem and you have a good thing going here. You can count on me."

With that settled the folksy smile gave way to the honest face full of concerned interest. "And how is the thing working out, son?"

"Well, you see, sir, we are just getting really started. The project has been going only a year or so. But already we think we are changing the image of the public library from that of the literary center of the middle class to that of a lively place with practical information for everyone including the functionally illiterate."

"Good," said Big John mechanically. "How have you done that?"

"We began with books about jobs and careers, training schools and colleges, and consumer-related materials—"

"But, son, how could that kind of stuff help the disadvantaged? Some of them can't read, you know. And a lot of them don't have money to go to colleges. What's more, many of them are on relief and when they go to the store to buy food and clothing, they don't really have much choice as consumers."

"You're right, sir. We soon found that out. Most of our books were geared to the middle class and folks did not even look at them. So we condensed some of this higher-reading-level stuff and rewrote it in simpler language, and we got some stuff from the Government Printing Office and from State agencies which seemed more practical."

"Good idea," murmured Big John. "How did it go?"

"Well, people began to look at our material, and in some centers they have borrowed materials. The things from the Government Printing Office and the State agencies seem to be the most popular."

"That follows," nodded Big John.

"But we do have a problem with staffing. The people in the community centers are not library trained. They keep the books in order but they do not try to encourage people to look at them or to borrow them. Of course, they have a lot of other work to do to. What we really need is more staff and I hope it will be staff with library training. Of course, more staff will cost more money . . ."

Big John clucked sympathetically.

"We need more publicity too. Not so much newspapers and radio and television as word of mouth. You know, one person who has been helped telling another."

"Yes, I reckon you are right, son. How many people have you helped get jobs?"

"I'm sorry, sir, but I really don't know. There must be some but we have not tried to keep records. I feel sure we have made some inroads, but most new, experimental services are not immediate, smashing successes, you know . . ." His voice trailed into silence.

"I see, son." Big John's voice was silken. "Well, keep up the good work. Reading means training and training means jobs and jobs fill hungry mouths. Like the Good Book says: Reading maketh a full man."

"But, sir . . ."

"Yes, son?"

"Thank you, sir, for your encouragement." Just in time he had remembered that a young man with a mission does not try to repair a Governor's quotations.

"It's been real nice talking with you, son." Big John strode back to the long black car.

Remember the First of April

On this, the Day of the Fool, I invite you to ponder a foolish question: Who is the Fool?

Ask a foolish question, you get . . . Could be. We shall see.

We begin with some words only a little less famous than the Gettysburg address: "It will take a classifier between five and ten minutes to assign a Dewey number to a title. (I have not made a careful time-study of this matter, but, to quote the distinguished American philosopher Lawrence P. Berra, 'You can observe a lot just by watching.') At this rate, assuming the classifier is paid $3 per hour, the cost of classifying one title lies somewhere between 25 and 50 cents. An average cost of 35 cents per title would be a fairly conservative estimate . . . How much time is required to classify a title previously cataloged by LC? . . . Ordinarily . . . only as much time as is required to copy the call number on the flyleaf of the book: about ten seconds. The average cost is about one cent. (This figure based on my own experience . . .)" (*LJ* 89 (1964) 2287-2291).

Now look carefully at these words of Librarianship's Angry Young Man. Bite each as you would a coin to test its truth. Is each word hard and firm as a genuine half dollar— or does it yield like mush wherever your teeth bear down? How far would you trust your surgeon's knife if it cut where facts like these directed?

In the World of the Box "Things go better with Coke."
In the World of the Book "Things go better with LC."

And yet. Think of our own old fashioned slogans before
the Angry Young Man flamed across the sullen sky.

"Keeping pace with knowledge." "Integrity of numbers."
Slogans to rally round. Slogans to fight and bleed and die
for. Slogans short only of "Mother Love." Each, like the
slogan of the Angry Young Man, is true. Each is also false.

Who wears the cap of the jester? Our Angry Young
Man? Or you and I?

Now let's go way out. Hear the Great Prophet of the East
and *his* call for change in classification. His verities multiply
like rabbits and they switch about in our hands like Proteus.

Grab two of the Prophet's verities if you can: Faceted
Classification and Personality.

Faceted Classification, we are told and told and told, is
good for you. Why is it good? Because it is "helpful," that's
why. And the proof that it is "helpful"? Hard, cold facts—
have you ever seen or heard them? Proof that the elusive
user does indeed find it "helpful"? Proof even that it is
new and not instead older than Dewey? Have you ever
seen it?

Or take a look at Personality. Have you ever heard anyone tell in precise, everyday language what Personality
really means? Can you hope that people will classify alike
until they do all mean the same thing by the word?

"Things go better with Colon." Is our Great Prophet
serious? Or does he only mock us?

Who wears the motley, my friend?

But let's get out of the tedious world of technical services
into the glamor land of reader services.

"Public Library Standards went that-a-way" (*LJ* 91
(1966)3864). They did indeed. But where had they come
from? Out of a series of careful, scientific studies of how
libraries could be most useful? Or out of the dreams of a

batch of men and women sitting around a table and talking about Tomorrow? Where did you come from, baby dear? Out of the everywhere into the here.

Where do the Standards for any kind of library come from?

Do Standards face the facts of life? Take one point alone: Manpower as shown in the table in *The Journal of Education for Librarianship* 7(1966)44. A gap of well over 100,000 librarians. There are only some 30,000 librarians in ALA; where shall we find so many more in this world or in the next?

Are Standards truly standards: Something to live by? Or are they only promotion gimmicks? Have we here only our ancient slogan: "Things go better with Libraries"?

Now let's talk of branch libraries. The April 1966 issue of *Library Trends* talked of them.

Look over the book with care. Bite each word as you bit the words of the Angry Young Man. You will find here much about *what* people are doing in branches differently from what they once did. But how much do you find about *why* they do it differently? Well, why *do* they do it differently? Because a series of experiments has showed in hard, cold facts of usefulness that what they do now is better? Or because someone guessed it was time to change? Can we even fall back on the argument: "Experience shows it works"? How many of the authors are currently branch librarians?

Do we have here only another antique slogan: "Things go better with Change"?

Slogans! But why not? Use your common sense; get the job done. The earth is flat; look out your window and see it. Why bother to prove the obvious? Do something useful. Think how many unicorns you can tame to man's service if you do not fritter away your time trying to find out if the world is really flat.

"What is Truth?" said jesting Pilate and would not stay for an answer. We librarians march with Pilate.

Have we a profession? Or only a mythology?

On the Day of the Fool whom do we celebrate?

Rosemary's Baby: You Name It

The baby has more pedigrees—every one of them blue rib-
bon—than a mongrel dog. That is why all the doting relatives, the sisters and the cousins and the aunts, cannot even
agree to describe the child, let alone name it.

Here is how one relative describes the infant: It is the
"entire continuum of information transfer—that is, the
flow or handling of information from the writing of literature by an author; through its editing, printing, publishing,
and distribution by the publisher; through indexing, abstracting, and distribution in reference journals; through
acquisition, organization, storage, and promotion of use in
an information center; and through its use by another
author and, perhaps, the production of new literature"—
John F. Harvey in *Annual Review of Information Science
and Technology* 2(1967)422.

Writing, Editing, Printing and Publishing, Indexing and
Abstracting, Library Science, Writing again—what a batch
of pedigrees! More parts than a jig-saw puzzle, more claims
than a medicine man.

As to a name: For a while they called him (or her)
"Documentation"; but the in-name now is more and more
"Information Science"—or "Information Sciences." (It all
depends on the point of view, no doubt: Do we have a fist
full of roses and dandelions and poison ivy—or do we hold
a bouquet?)

Only on one thing can the relatives agree: The new child, in spite of the bar sinister on its classy coat of arms, is far classier than its stodgy old cousin Library Science.

It seems that we are in the very middle of an explosion— an explosion of information. And Library Science, poor old thing, cannot tell an explosion from a hole in a book. Indeed, she stubbornly insists on clinging to books—codex books at that, mind you—long after the now-thing is not books or even periodicals or even non-book materials but the thing that is in them: Information, of course. How can Library Science be so stupid? Even her best friends ask her.

Now Information Science will be really bright. She will look for each bit of information, not for carriers of information—for Microthought, not Macrothought. And then she will put that tiny Microthought exactly where it will always be found *every* time *anybody ever* looks for it again. It is really easy. Information Science, you see, will not sit around, clinging to old fashioned catalog cards and book shelving devices. She will just dance in with arms full of facets and computers and — whizz, there it will be all fixed up before you can say "Melvil." At least, that is the way it will be if we stick to Information Science till she grows up and shakes out all the bugs. And then the explosion will fade away with the bugs.

Grandma's attic will no longer be a mess: every tiny Microthought will be in its own little corner on its own little toes. All you need do will be to punch your console and the Microthought of your choice will come running.

But will you get "it" or "them"? Will Information Science find duplicate Microthoughts just as Library Science finds duplicate books? What is our explosion really like? Is it even an explosion of ideas? Or is it often an explosion of words? In the old fashioned world of Library Science how many novels have the same plot? How many non-fiction books re-state the same facts? In the brand new world of Information Science how many books on Information Science itself differ from all the rest? How many of the articles which cram the journals differ completely from all that has gone before?

It is true that we do face a crisis. But is it really all that different from other crises? Crisis faced Putnam in the Library of Congress; crisis faced Panizzi in the British Museum; crisis faced Bodley and James; crisis faced Callimachus. Many books, many words, many ideas slipped through their fingers and we had them no longer.

It is true that today the job is infinitely bigger; but today the work force is also infinitely bigger. It is true that today the printing press grinds infinitely faster; but today we have also the computer so we can sort infinitely faster. Even so, no doubt, many books, many words, many ideas will slip through our fingers and we shall have them no more. They will have to be re-thought, re-discovered, re-written.

Perhaps it will be just as well. Suppose Information Science had succeeded from the beginning. Suppose everything that was ever written and everything that was ever thought had survived. The Information Science of yesterday's Information Science of the day before yesterday's Information Science of the day before that day's Information Science would give even a computer mental constipation.

Is it really unbearable to re-think some things, re-discover some things, re-write some things? The re-done things might even be better than the first.

Is Information Science a fact or is it only another dream of perfection? Will it lead to perfection or will it lead to hysteria because we cannot face up to all its demands? Is Information Science a science or is it only an alchemy or an astrology? Is it a collection or is it only a conglomeration? Is it a baby or only a patchwork rag doll?

Is Information Science Rosemary's Baby or is it Raggedy Ann?

The Cooking of a Goose

Trueman J. Upman beamed on the expectant upturned faces of his staff around the big table.

"They did it!" He boomed the glad tidings a second time: "They did it! Square Grove Library is the very first public library in the country with a Library Bill of Rights written right into the city ordinances. The Council voted it last night. Not a single vote opposed. They said some real nice things too about the Librarian (Upman always referred to himself in the third person; it seemed more modest) for wanting it—and, of course, they said some nice things about the Library too."

Upman's beam melted into a frown. That faint smile on the edges of Deffer's face. Of course, it *was* the Circulation Librarian who had been first to suggest the idea; but it had taken some one who could talk up to the Council to put it over. Deffer ought to realize . . . With an effort Upman turned on the beam again.

"I'm sure mighty thankful to all of you for your suggestions about how we could handle censorship, and I'm sure you are all glad now that the Censor's goose is cooked once and for all."

"How does the Statement go, True?" Gafferand, the Assistant Librarian, knew how it went because he had drafted it, but he also knew Upman was bursting to read it.

"Well, the thing is not really very long or fancy." Upman could never resist modesty. "There are three parts to the Statement. The first is like this: As a function of library services, books and all other material selected should be chosen for values of interest, information, and enlightenment of all members of the community."

Upman paused as if for applause. Deffer's smile burst into a grin. "A splendid first statement, sir. They would have to vote for *that*. Be like voting against mother love if they did not. Sort of a Trojan horse approach. Get them into the habit of voting yes and then sock it to them."

Upman frowned again. These young smart guys the library schools were turning out nowadays!

"I'm a little bothered by the exact meaning." Miss Crumby's quaver broke in on Upman's meditation. She *would* talk about exact meanings, a reference librarian. "Does it mean that everything we have must be useful to everybody in the town? 'All' is a big word, sir."

"Please, Miss Crumby, let's not quibble. I suppose it *could* be taken to mean what you suggest but only if you strain at it. It's just a simple, straightforward statement really. If we insist on your meaning, we couldn't buy much of anything."

"That's what I mean, sir." Miss Crumby's quaver faded into Upman's sonorous sweep into the Second Part.

"In no case should materials be excluded because of the race or nationality or the social, political, or religious views of the authors."

"Then we get to buy all those books the Afro-American Center has been asking for." Deffer's voice was jubilant and his grin had lost its trace of a leer.

Upman's mouth fell open. Last night he had agreed with one member of the Council to go a bit slow with those commies in the Afro-American group; they were out only to make trouble. The case had seemed so clear then. He started to demur; then he closed his mouth. Best wait till Deffer suggested specific books. Then he could find something; perhaps they would be shown to be without "interest, information and enlightenment for *all*." Perhaps Miss Crumby had a point—bless her quaver!

Upman was content for now to say simply: "Of course, we shall have to look at the budget as we would for all other large purchases."

It was Deffer's turn to look meditative, Upman noted with satisfaction. He went on to the Third Part:

"No library materials should be proscribed or removed from the libraries because of partisan or doctrinal disapproval."

"That means the Legion for True Democracy can't ask us to get rid of our books against the Vietnam War, doesn't it?" Deffer's voice was almost pleading.

"Well . . . it depends. Would you call the Legion for True Democracy 'partisan or doctrinal'?"

Upman did not really mean to quibble. It was just that this problem had not occurred to him last night in the flush of victory.

Deffer did not mean to quibble either: "The Legion qualifies on both counts, sir. But, if we have to go to all the trouble to prove in black and white before a court of law that disapproval is partisan or doctrinal—why, that would take years and years."

"I'm sure it will not be all that difficult." Upman's voice was not all that sure.

"Is that all there is to the Statement, sir?"

"Why—yes, that's all." What did the young whippersnapper want now?

"There is nothing in the Statement about obscenity and pornography and you remember all the trouble we have had with that. Just last week the Legion of Purity started a campaign to cut our budget because we won't let them check our book orders before we send them in."

For once Upman had nothing to say. Legions of Woe sat on his brow.

The Day of the Worm-Free World

Do you remember yesterday? The day when we lived in the best of all possible worlds?

You had a nice swell job in a real live-wire profession (it is a profession; it says so itself). You got to sit and read books and meet a lot of nice people and you got to get them to read a lot of books and enjoy them with you. You got a nice swell salary.

And there were the fringe benefits. You got machines to do all the dirty work; all you had to do was to sit and use the old brain. That is, of course, if you had an old brain to use—and if you didn't have the brain, all you had to do was sit. You got a lot of pretty girls to work with. Unless, of course, you were one of the pretty girls yourself—but that made it even better because you could pick one of those nice young men who came to sit with you and look at all the books—an engineer or a dentist or a plumber perhaps. (You would not want to be hooked for life with a librarian would you, one of those creeps you had to put up with at work?)

Yes, yesterday was great, truly great, and the greatest thing of all about it is that it is still here. Yesterday was the best of all possible worlds except. Except that now and then a worm peeped out of the library apple at you. You didn't have to swallow it if you kept your eyes open—eyeball to eyeball confrontation and that was the end of that for the time.

We poured out our tale of worms to our Washington Lobby and the Lobby poured out the tale of woe to the Congress and the Congress poured out pails of cash to us —well, to some of us—to find worm smashers. *Library Journal* took inventory of a sample of the pails of cash in August 1967, p. 2691-2694.

That was moons and moons ago. Today is surely Tomorrow. The worm smasher hunters must have spent all that cash long since. No doubt they found what they hunted. No doubt at all. Smash, smash, smash, the worms were smashing. We greet the dawn of a new day, the Day of the Worm-Free World. No doubt. Just read a few items from the *LJ* list of long ago and rejoice at what your cash must have done for the worms by now.

The Smashers of Worms must be legion by now:

Item: Did college students burn you? Today they just tune in on the "dial access communication system" and bring the library to desks in their dormitory rooms; and before them is laid out all they want to know and more— even while they go on with that dice-and-bull-and-beer session with the guys and dolls. All this you got, my friend, for only 64 grand.

Item: Now they can use that computer to index and inventory geological and biological specimens in that IMC we call the Smithsonian. The pail of cash for that: less than 300 grand—a real bargain.

Item: Now you know all about people who work in libraries: How to pick them, how to catch them, how to train them. That came to 235 grand, ma'am. Cheap at half the price; it may even catch a real groovy male librarian for you after all.

Item: How to get the biggest and best library service to people in a rapidly expanding area? Now we know for only

104 grand. Must have been lower priority than how to catch librarians, but we have it anyway for whatever it may be worth.

Item: Worry no more about how automation will change library architecture, "personnel deployment" (what big words you use, grandma), and the development of systems applicable to other large libraries. One guess is as good as another, but 417 grand must have made it more good. Why, sure.

Item: They set up and tested an "information processing laboratory for education and research in library science." It took only 141 grand and it will do a world of good, we are all sure.

Item: Do you know the difference between "knowledge" and a "data file"? Sure you do! Well, if you don't this will, no doubt, ring a bell: "Cognitive Memory—an Epistemological Approach to Information Storage and Retrieval." Now, see, you did know all the time! That will be a real worm smasher and you got it all for only 250 grand.

Item: It took only a measly 7500 smackers to find out how to convert complex subject headings so they can be meaningfully arranged by fully mechanical means. More means than smackers there. Oh well: do a little job and you get only a little cash. Next time these folks ask for cash I bet they use bigger words.

Item: Now they know how to teach "working scientists" how to use information tools, techniques, resources, and facilities created for their benefit. (How about the scientists who don't work? Getting the unemployed to read— seems like that should be a good library problem too. Maybe a juicy project for you, my friend, if the government ever goes into the business again.) Anyway, work on the working scientists got almost 30 grand; we are coming up from the depths of subject headings.

Item: Now we know how to turn over that blasted reserve desk to a friendly little old computer, no doubt. You can join the boys in the back stacks and use your brain for the better things of life (like a friendly little old card game?). Anyway, 35 grand on that one—cheap enough.

All these great and wonderful worm smashers—and many another—were promised yesterday and, no doubt, they have come to pass by now. And where did all the grand grands come from? Well, where do you think? You ought to know, friend. Have you checked your wallet recently?

Even the worm-free world has its price.

The Debugging of Victor Hugo

Once upon a time only potato vines were debugged. You could do it with your fingers one bug at a time. Or you could do it with Paris green and a water sprinkler—a mass production job. From that age of innocence we have long since slipped into an age of sophistication and we have learned to debug anything: machines, systems, theories. Even poetry.

We shall now debug a poem: "Victor Hugo on the and records and realia? Perhaps even in that bleak long-ago Burning of a Library, Juin 1871," published in *Wilson Library Bulletin*, June 1969, pages 980-981, and, no doubt, in many another notable place. We shall, of course, all be the better for it; normally such a state follows debugging.

The poem begins and ends as follows:
place. After all, where else could he borrow all those films day the only-book library *deserved* to be burned.

> " 'Tis you then burned the library?
> I did,
> I brought the fire . . .
> I cannot read."

All this is pretty straight stuff and we can dismiss the rioting burner (even if he is a Communist) with the melancholy reflection that had it only been the day of the multi-media center instead of the only-book library he would, no doubt, have spared the building and its contents as a holy

But now we consider the three dots in the third line of the quotation above. Those three dots mark the omitted part of the poem, the part to be debugged, all 55 lines of it. Those 55 lines are the outcry of Philo Biblon (dubbed P. B. by his friends and friends of the library) and in his frenzy he thinks the burner reads.

"Wretch!" he screams (P. B. is really fond of "Wretch" and " 'Tis") "Wretch, 'tis your own torch which you have just put out!" (Apparently the non-reader burner knew enough to fight fire with fire.) P. B. rushed on: The Book, he proclaims, is "the Master's bugbear" and the Book "has ever taken side with you." The Book "speaks; the Slave and Pariah disappear."

This may be news for the non-reader burner; for a reader burner it would be a shock. For he would always have thought otherwise. Apart from *Uncle Tom's Cabin* and a few other books and newspapers in the 19th century and the outburst of books in the 1960's, how often did the Book attack the Master? How often, instead, did the Book paper over the sins of the Master?

Of course, in 1871 it may be that the non-reader burner was not black. Even so, how many books other than those by Marx, Hugo, Dickens, and other cranks bothered about the plight of the non-reader white burner in the flourishing days of the 19th century industrial empire building? What did they offer more than communist dogma or sentimental humanitarianism? Even our own patron Saint Andrew Carnegie had his Homestead Massacre to explain away if he could.

But P. B. is a persistent cuss. The burner, he shrieks, flings his flaming torch "into this mine of Bibles and all this heap divine—dread Aeschylus, Homer, and Job upright against the horizon, Molière, Voltaire and Kant" and all these "you set on fire!" Here is, indeed, a mixed bag. The Bible's ability to set free—or to bind—is almost infinite.

Aeschylus and Job debated with God about the fate of man; Homer wrote in lofty verse of kings and noble lords who fought about a woman; Molière, Voltaire, and Kant were in one way or another (as P. B. shouts) liberators—but liberators of the mind. Nothing in the bag helped noticeably to "undermine the gallows, war, and famine."

Nor does P. B. help the case when he drags in his second crew: Plato, Beccaria, Milton, Dante, Shakespeare, and Corneille. "Shall not their great souls waken yours in you? Dazzled you feel the same as each of them; reading you grow more gentle, pensive, grave." News and more news for the burner, be he reader or non-reader. "Gentle, pensive, grave—how come I burned the joint if I am all those things?" (Hugo forgot to record the question.)

But P. B. grows not weary in well doing. Books, he announces, bring you Science; they bring Liberty. "The Book's your wealth! The Book means Truth, Knowledge and Duty, Virtue, Progress, Right, and Reason scattering hence delirious dream." (Also, P. B., what of Motherhood and the Kitchen Sink?) Perhaps the burner could really read after all. Perhaps it is only a desperate lunge at escape when he bursts out "I cannot read" and leaves poor P. B. with his mouth hanging open.

Poor P. B.! But why poor P. B. What more have you and I to offer as the library burns? "Be all you can be. Read!" "Explore Inner Space. Read!" National Library Week. Books are good for you. What more, indeed?

In the year that New York City cut its library budget $3.3 million, New York State, through its Urban Education Fund, gave the New York City Board of Education $5 million to start some adult learning centers (See *Wilson Library Bulletin*, June 1969, page 944). In that same year federal cash for libraries dwindled and library budgets crumbled. Libraries we had never built were burning. We screamed as loudly as P. B. screamed—and gave as little reason.

Victor Hugo, they say, thought Paris should be renamed "Hugo." It may be we should rename the United States "Libraria."

The debugging of Victor Hugo is now concluded. Next?

The Future Is What We Make It

"What we have here," said the Dean to the Candidate for the Doctoral Program, "is a future-oriented school." He paused for the pronouncement to sink in.

The Candidate squirmed in his future-oriented chair and hoped that the future-oriented curriculum was more comfortable than the chair. He smiled sympathetically and murmured: "What of the present and the past, sir? Can we hope to foresee or understand the future if we do not know something of the past and the present? Will not the future grow out of them?"

The Dean frowned. "The future will grow out of the past and the present only if we let it. That, young man, is the point. If the future grows out of the past and the present it will be as traditional and as conservative as they are. We cannot let that happen can we?"

The Candidate gulped; then he plunged ahead: "What is the nature of the future if it is not the product of today and yesterday? And how shall we know that the future is *not* the product of today and yesterday if we have not discovered precisely what today and yesterday are?"

The Dean's frown deepened. Why did this Young Man come so highly recommended? Surely he could only make trouble. Then he smiled triumphantly: "It all depends, young man, on the difference between Acquiry and Inquiry."

The Young Man shuddered slightly inside; he also had read Professor Graper's article in last month's *Library Teacher's Journal*. Spoken aloud, the jargon offended him even more than it had on paper. But he managed a polite question: "Inquiry and Acquiry? What do you mean by that, sir?"

The Dean mellowed; perhaps the Young Man was doctoral material after all. "Well, you see, it's like this: A school can teach what is known and what libraries think is practical. Probably this is all that the libraries of the country want us to do. If a school teaches these facts, then the student simply *Acquires* them and can use them. This is Acquiry and the product of such teaching will be conservative and traditional."

"I see," smiled the Young Man. "And what is Inquiry?"

The Dean smiled even more broadly. A pretty sharp young man after all. He sailed into his exposition: "Well, you see, a graduate school must also be theoretical; it must discover the *unknown*; it must ask questions about the known; it must experiment; it must discover the inter-relationship of librarianship with other disciplines. To ask questions about the known; to experiment: this is *Inquiry* and it will make a future which will be untraditional and unconventional."

"I believe I understand." The Young Man was deferential. "Inquiry is something like what Socrates had in mind when he said he was a gadfly to the state because he went around asking questions about what men thought to be true."

The Dean gulped. Had this brazen young man tried to trap him? "Well," he spoke slowly, "If you put it that way, I suppose it may be about that way." He frowned; this was not coming out the way he had wanted to say it at all. "But Socrates was a long time ago and things are changed now; we must live in the future, not the past, you know."

"You are quite right, sir." The Young Man spoke rapidly; somehow he must try to close this gap; after all, the School had a pretty good reputation in spite of its "future-oriented" curriculum; and he supposed that you had to take a certain amount of guff in *any* school. "Socrates did, indeed, live a long time ago. But, excuse me, sir. You were explaining about Acquiry and Inquiry and I interrupted."

The Dean was a bit mollified; but he was still suspicious. Nonetheless, he pushed ahead. "A true graduate school and a good doctoral program must be theoretical, it must stress Inquiry, not Acquiry, it must communicate the nature of its objectives and discoveries to the library profession. In short, it must, as I said before, be future-oriented and it must change the nature of the library profession. This is what Acquiry and Inquiry mean in our program. Do you think you understand such a concept, and is it something you can live and work with?"

Both men knew that the Young Man did, indeed, understand. Neither was convinced that the Young Man could live and work with the idea on the Dean's terms. In spite of his eagerness to please, the Young Man heard himself murmur a question: "But, sir, can you have Inquiry without Acquiry? Can you know what questions to ask unless you know and understand the facts and assumptions by which practicing librarians live?"

The Dean grew more suspicious, but he managed to keep his cool. "If you put it that way, I suppose you are right." He grunted. Somehow it seemed to him he had said that before not too long ago.

Horror gripped the Young Man. He had muffed it. Now he must do something and do it in a hurry. "All I mean to say, sir, is that we are ourselves largely the product of the past and the present and if we know and understand the facts of librarianship in the terms of the past and the present it may be that the future librarianship we build will be in a large measure the product of the past and the present no matter how we do it."

The Dean frowned and the Young Man rushed to his conclusion: "And, you see, sir, if we truly believe in Inquiry as a way of life we must be willing to ask questions even about Inquiry itself."

"Very interesting." The Dean wore his fixed smile. "It is good to have had this little chat with you. I shall let you know our decision next week." The Dean's fixed smile was still there and he shook the Young Man's hand, but his heart was heavy. Somewhere, somehow he would have to find one more doctoral student if he was to use all the government fellowships he had asked for and received.

The future looked bleak.

The Morning After the Week Before

On Monday morning after Midwinter Q. Barker Byte reported to his staff meeting on the progress of the revolution in the National Library Association. Somehow Barky had never yet been able to work travel money for staff into the library budget, and he felt it his duty as an alert administrator to keep them informed about what they had missed.

Barky was proud of his reputation as a progressive in NLA, and he had zealously gone to every meeting on the "Interim Report of the Activities Committee on New Directions for NLA," and his comments in those meetings had been long and loud and often. Now every member of his staff clutched a xerox copy of the report and Barky asked them to read it over; then they would discuss it. Barky liked to have staff discuss general professional questions. It was democratic—made them feel that they were part of big things. Also it was good for staff morale to get their minds off daily problems and local complaints.

Barky's staff read obediently and in silence until Quentin Punch broke in: "I see they have all the in-words: 'relevant' and 'meaningful' and 'priorities for action.' Good old NLA. Keeps up to date on words anyway."

Barky frowned but once more he remembered to be grateful for the library's retirement system; no more of Quent's disruptive remarks after this year. He smiled and turned on a positive remark.

"I like the statement later on which points out that this report rests on the NLA statement of purpose 'to promote library service and librarianship' because this purpose implies that 'librarianship is not an end in itself but finds its justification in the service it renders to society.' As the needs of society change so must the service priorities of the library change . . ."

"So what else is new?" Quent was on the air again. "Seems to me, Barky, that all this is simply a statement of the obvious. Anyway, how could a revolution of any relevance (to coin a word) *rest* on an NLA statement of purpose out of the distant past?"

"Oh, Quentin, you are just being picky!" Miss Amelia Packer was of the Old Guard on the library staff, but she did not care for Quentin Punch. "Every revolution grows out of the past and you know it."

Quent grinned and Barky moved in quickly:

"Let's look at the list of current priorities. I particularly like it that they have made Social Responsibilities Priority A. This is an area in which we have not been aggressive enough, I suspect. We have taken care of the bibliographical responsibility in the first paragraph pretty well in this library, but how about the list of problems and duties in the second paragraph?"

"Mr. Byte, I think it is a very good list of the problems facing us all today—runs all the way from population increase through Vietnam and Biafra to pollution." Randall McGoo was fresh out of library school and only last year he had made an A in a course in "Social Functions of the Library." "I am mighty glad to see the NLA say at last that it has an obligation to 'support and help defend' librarians who work to solve these problems. That would have been a big help for Tommy Pane last month."

Barky winced. Tommy Pane had joined in a march led by the Black Panthers and Barky had had one devil of a

time with the trustees even after Tommy proved so ineffi-
cient at his job that Barky had to let him go. Barky opened
his mouth and then closed it. Perhaps best to let Randy's
remark go too.

"One thing I don't like is the statement that NLA
'should be willing to take a position for the guidance and
support of its members on current critical issues.'" Miss
Packer had joined the fray again. "'Support' I can understand and I suppose if NLA is going to insist on taking a
stand on such things NLA *should* support its members in
the stand. But 'guidance'? No one—not even a high powered
NLA—is going to guide me in what I think about anything." Miss Packer glared and Quentin Punch grinned.
Barky writhed. Somehow these things had all seemed so
good and so simple last week.

"Let's move on to Manpower, Priority B." Barky hoped
this one would bring out the silent majority; surely there
would be no trouble here.

"Well, I for one agree when it says that NLA should be
neither purely an educational organization nor an organization only to benefit its members. We need to do both jobs
in NLA and we shall have our hands full if we do just that."
Barky smiled happily. Good old Smitty Butterfeld. You
could always count on him. Too bad he had never wanted
to leave the charging desk.

"One thing strikes me as a bit curious." Quentin Punch
had an innocent and inquiring smile. "The statement says
that if we are to 'compete for recruits with the many other
professions that serve society' we cannot afford incompe-
tence or inferior status or rewards. If there are so many
other people rushing in to solve these problems, then why
all the urgency about librarians getting into the act? Will
these other people solve the problems anyway even if we
just stick to being librarians?"

"You know, Quentin, that is rather strange now that you

put it that way." Miss Packer suddenly decided she did care for Quentin Punch. She turned to Barky. "Another thing bothers me, Mr. Byte. On the next page it tells us to develop a public relations program to improve our status. Is *that* how librarians will get status? Sell us like cans of beans or Fords? What of all the talk we hear all the time about service—even in *this* document?"

Barky was almost glad when Randy burst in again:

"What I can't understand is what they say about the library schools. First on page 3 it says library schools should 'screen applicants more carefully' and a little later it calls for recruitment of 75,000 young men and women into the profession. Screen and recruit! That screen will need some mighty big holes!"

"Probably you are right, Randy," smiled Barky. "We do want to get the job done, but we must have an eye out for quality in performance too."

Priority C was Intellectual Freedom, but Barky remembered Tommy Pane. "Let's look at Priority D—Legislation. What with the government cutting back on funds for education, this will be important, I think you will have to admit."

"I suppose you're right, Mr. Byte." Miss Packer was not really convinced. "But I don't see anything in this section about appropriations to help public libraries. In fact, sir, there is nothing revolutionary here. Even the request for more cash is old."

"And Priority E—Planning, Research and Development— is in one sense just a part of Priority D—Legislation." Quent had seized the ball again and he ran down the field. "I'm not entirely sure I like Priority E anyway. What do they mean when they say 'monitor research' performed under NLA sponsorship. That could easily mean a sort of censorship."

Barky gulped. "I suppose it could lead to that, Quent, but

surely you are just borrowing trouble on that point, I hope. Anyway I know that you will all agree to Priority F—Democratization of NLA and Alternative Patterns of Organization."

From the back of the room came a voice from the hitherto silent majority: "But, Mr. Byte, they say they are looking at the structure of NLA 'with a view to recommending economies,' and all they offer for democratization is to restrict the number of committees any guy can hold at one time . . ."

The door opened discreetly and Barky's secretary peeked in discreetly.

"Mr. Byte, I hate to bother you, but you have a phone call—someone in Washington and he says it is terribly important."

"Thank you, Miss Crete." Barky had never dreamed a day would come when he would be glad to hear his brother-in-law was in a new scrape.

Q. Barker Byte strode briskly from the room.

The Tabby Cat and the Elephant

Bibliography belongs in a circus. Bibliography is the tabby cat that grew into a tiger, the elephant that the blind men touched and described, the ass that patiently bears men's burdens and the ass that gallops madly through the hill wherever fancy leads.

All these things are true. Fredson Bowers' tabby cat-tiger is real; Bibliography has grown tremendously. Every man does describe Bibliography to fit his own needs and limitations; Verner Clapp's Bibliography in *Encyclopedia Americana* and Sir Walter Greg's Bibliography in the Biblographical Society's *Studies in Retrospect* (1945) are not the same animal at all. Finally, to some Bibliography is a handmaiden; to others she proclaims her independence as a "pure science." The tiger, it seems, is also a chameleon.

And yet, in life cats may grow into fat cats but never into tigers; an elephant is still an elephant though a blind toucher may call him a snake; and in the hills no less than in the barnyard an ass is still an ass.

What, then is Bibliography? Is she one or many? The specialists have worn blinders and they have had many words to use because they wrote books or articles. In one page or two I shall try once more. Perhaps cramped space will lead to fundamentals—or only into shallow water!

The basic meaning of Bibliography, "writing books," is long since obsolete. Convention has twisted this meaning into another: "Writing about books." This later meaning underlies most current definitions, particularly if we stretch "books" to mean any recorded information.

Now writing about books—or about anything—is no good if there is no reader. Probably people read only what they think useful. ("Useful" may mean many things: pleasure, information, stimulation—what not?) But even if what you write is useful only the most stubborn will read for long what they cannot easily understand.

Perhaps we have here the elements of a basic definition: Bibliography is writing about books; it makes books more useful; and it is in language easily understood.

How can you make a book more useful? The most you can do is to locate the book or something in it. You may locate the book as a physical object in relation to other physical objects; that is, you tell where to find it. Or you may locate a book in relation to other editions and issues of that book; that is, you tell what comes closest to what the author originally wrote. Finally, you may locate a book in relation to other writing on the same or related subjects; that is, you tell what it is about.

These seem to be the basic jobs of Bibliography. Every bibliographer does one or more of these jobs for one or more books. We name the bibliographer, however, (not for one of these three jobs but) for the area in which he works:

He may, for instance, try to locate all books in all three ways. This seemed possible only in the very long ago and in today's wildest dreams. We call this bibliographer a Universal Bibliographer. Or he may try to locate all the books in a particular library. We call him a Cataloger. Or he may try to locate all the books of a particular time or place or subject or form—what not? We call him a Subject Bibliographer or a Special Bibliographer.

Or he may, of course, find some area not listed above.

Convention sets our basic definition: "Writing about

books." Convention also deals with what we may call the "Quasi-bibliographers."

A commentary is, of course, "writing about books"; and, indeed, it may help to establish the subject of a book or determine the annotation to be made in a bibliography such as Winchell or the Pforzheimer catalog. But it is conventional not to call a commentary Bibliography.

An index certainly makes a book useful, but it is conventional in many quarters not to call an indexer a bibliographer.

A study of the printing history of a book helps determine editions and issues, and its writer is conventionally called a bibliographer. Often convention goes farther and calls him an analytical bibliographer or a descriptive bibliographer or an historical bibliographer. And yet—in spite of convention —these three terms are redundant. It is much as if we were to speak of "true truth." For all bibliographers—even the compilers of short-title bibliographies—can locate their books in relation to other physical objects, other editions and issues, and other subjects only if they go at their books analytically, historically and descriptively. Of course, the work of a student of the printing history of a book now and then determines such things as statements of collation and arrangement of issues in a printed bibliography. But a similar service, we have seen, did not win the title of bibliographer for the commentator.

Convention defines Bibliography. The Zealots shape its course.

Bibliography, by definition, involves a written record. *How* do you keep the record? For ordinary books: The Library of Congress printed cards and the successive editions of the ALA rules. For "rare" books: McKerrow, Greg, Bowers & Co. The tabby cat did indeed grow into a tiger under the watchful care of the Zealots of the Record. How to keep the record? With details, of course. How else?

But Bibliography is not merely a record. It is an *organized* record; it must be if it locates books in relation to other books and subjects. So the analytical bibliographer draws fine lines between "edition," "issue," and "state." Subject bibliographers work out fine-spun plans of classification and draw up newer and bigger subject heading lists. From macro-thought to micro-thought; from micro-cosmic bibliography to macro-cosmic bibliography. By now they begin to talk of Documentation and Social Epistemology and Information Science. How organize the record? In mystery, of course. How else?

The Zealot demands an answer to all possible needs of all possible users for all possible times.

But in these happy dreams of a brave new world we walk the edge of nightmare. For each Zealot views the others with profound distrust and some contempt.

The analytical bibliographer and the information scientist think catalogers are shallow, inaccurate, old-fashioned, wasteful of time and energy. The cataloger and the information scientist think the analytical bibliographer a pedantic and arty dabbler in trifles and pretty books. The analytical bibliographer is almost unaware of the information scientist's existence; and the cataloger thinks the information scientist an intellectual confidence man who has taken over as his own inventions what are established library practices and given them fancy names.

Circus indeed!

The War Without Blood

"Magnificent!" R. Casherton Bathose beamed across his big desk at the two students. " 'Contrary to our national and moral interests'—of course it is! The President had no business sending troops into Cambodia—and those poor kids at Kent State! I repeat: It is magnificent, this statement you students and faculty at Thornybrook have drawn up. Library Schools have sure changed since I was a student. Nothing but good old Dewey Decimals and reader service then. Thornybrook is in today's world. Relevant. That's the word: Relevant!"

Jack and Nancy smiled. "We're glad you like the statement, sir."

"Well, by George, I certainly do like it. Magnificent, I say! I like what you're doing too. Closing school but not going on strike. Going out to work against the War and this Cambodia business. Anything I can do to help?"

"Well, sir, that's why we're here. We should like to have permission to put up some posters—"

"Why, of course, Jack. Put up as many as you like." A shadow slid across Cashy's face. "You will understand, however, that if anyone wants to put up posters on the other side of the question we shall have to let them do it. We have some strong veterans' groups in this town and they are taxpayers too, you know."

"We understand, sir." Nancy smiled sweetly. "One more

thing, sir. We'd like to have you give free time to any of the younger members of your staff who would be willing to help us get signatures on the petition."

"Petition." Cashy's face froze. "What petition?"

"Why, it's the statement you have in your hand, sir. The final paragraph demands that we get out of Vietnam at once and end the war. We hope to get a lot of signatures in Chugville."

Cashy had glanced only at the first paragraph; he now read the last. He was amazed. "Why, you kids are really serious about this, aren't you?"

"Yes, sir. We are quite serious." Jack frowned. "There's really no point in just closing school, sir, if we don't use the time to do something about the War. We have staked our reputation and our time for study on this project. We are, indeed, serious."

Cashy had recovered his smile. "I'm with you 100 per cent, I want you to understand that."

"We understand." They smiled again. "So you will grant our request!—"

"No, I'm afraid I can't grant the request, much as I'd like to." Cashy looked out the big window and hurried on. "You see we've a big bond issue to be voted on next month and we've got to win it or we can't build that new branch in the ghetto. Lots of folks in this town don't like the war but they don't want to get out dishonorably. That petition would polarize opinion. If Library staff were back of it, we'd lose the bond issue for sure. Even if the staff were willing to carry the petition on their own time it would hurt the Library. You do understand, don't you?" Cashy's voice was pleading.

Jack and Nancy rose. "Yes sir, we understand."

"Good for Old Thornybrook!" The President of the National Library Association beamed across his big desk at the two students. "A really stirring statement. And you're not just talking about it. You're doing something. Magnificent!"

Sue and Sam smiled. "We're glad you like the statement, sir."

"Well, of course, I like it. Anything I can do to help?"

"There is one thing, sir." Sue smiled even more brightly. "The students are down at Washington visiting their Senators and Representatives to ask them to stop the granting of money for the war—"

"Good tactics!" The President of the National Library Association was always impressed by action in young people; he always mentioned it favorably in the speeches he was having to make this year.

Sue brushed over the interruption. "What we'd like for you to do, sir, would be to endorse on behalf of the NLA all candidates for Congress who oppose the Vietnam War. Here's a list of them we compiled these last two days." She laid the paper before him.

The President spoke very slowly: "Well, you see, I'm not really authorized to speak for the NLA on a political issue; even on a professional issue I should have to have the support of the entire membership. For an endorsement such as this we should need action at the membership meeting this summer—"

The President began to look over the list. "You really put the NLA on the spot here." He frowned. "For instance, the very first name you have here is Al Corumber. Now he is opposed to Senator Zobor; and Zobor, it is true, is a fanatic on this war thing—son killed in Vietnam and all that. But Senator Zobor has backed every bit of library legislation we have ever proposed. We could not possibly endorse his opponent; why, we don't even have any idea of where Corumber stands on libraries. You can, of course, force action on this list at membership meeting but I doubt very much if it would be adopted."

"Do you mean, sir, that NLA wants money for library projects more than it wants to take a stand on a moral issue?" Sam's anger blazed and Sue was white.

"That's a rather extreme way to put it, son." The President was truly sorry. They were both so very young. "Is there anything else I can do?"

"No—not now!" Sam had won back his cool. "There was one other thing: We were going to ask that you have the NLA Congressional Lobby work for peace, but I guess that would get the same answer. If the NLA Lobby worked for peace it would anger hawkish congressmen and lose cash for NLA projects."

"I'm afraid you are correct."

Suddenly the NLA President felt old and tired.

Wagon Full of Maize

Do not hang your head and sneak away, friend. You do too have a Code of Ethics. Just like the Doctors—the M.D.'s, that is.

And just like the Doctors' Code, your Code was not born yesterday. It goes all the way back to December 1938. Sort of a Christmas present, even if it was in ancient times just like the Doctors' Code.

And yet, your Code is not really like the Doctors' Code. Why should it be? *You* do not cut people up, do you?

It was not some Greek foreigner who invented your Code; it was a batch of 100 per cent Americans with 100 per cent American names and 100 per cent American ideas. Perhaps that is why no one has ever called your Code "Communist" or "Communist-inspired." Perhaps your Code is why the House Un-American Activities Committee has never called you before it.

Another thing: Your Code does not monkey around with ideals and all that jazz. It gets down to brass tacks in a hurry. Your Code tells you right off that the library "exists for the benefit of a given constituency." How much brass tackier could you get? Too bad they did not have your Code around for a model when they wrote the Declaration of Independence.

When you join the library world you "assume an obligation"; your Code says so. Something like when you join a church. What is your "obligation"? Your Code gets real spiritual here. You are to "maintain ethical standards of behavior" toward (1) "the governing authority" under which you work, (2) the "library constituency" (strange that the constituency is only No. 2 if the library exists *for* it, but why be picky?), (3) "the library as an institution" and your "fellow workers on the staff," (4) other librarians wherever they may be, and (5) "society in general." In this long catalog what happened to the kitchen sink? But, as I said: Do not be picky; your Code is real spiritual. You already have a Quintet instead of just a Trinity; what more do you want?

Your Code is impartial: It takes care of your boss as well as you. He is to "keep the governing authority informed on professional standards and progressive action." What of retrogressive action? Well, what of it?

Are you loyal to your boss, friend? You should be; it is in the Code. But do not worry. "Whenever the good of the service requires a change in personnel, timely warning should be given"; and, if necessary, "unsatisfactory service should be terminated in accordance with the policy of the library and the rules of tenure." So if you are fired, friend, it will be a firing with dignity and solemnity. A real comforting thing to keep in mind. Why, your Code will not even call it firing.

Your Code says a lot of other nice things about the "governing authority"; but let's move on to the "library constituency." Your Code says you will keep "in touch" with the constituency. How do you keep in touch? Take a Gallup Poll, maybe? Well, anyway, once you touch the constituency you buy a lot of books and stuff (your Code says "acquire materials") to meet the constituency's need. (I should confess that I have indulged in textual criticism here. The text, perhaps because it is so ancient, is quite corrupt at this point. The sentence begins with something about your boss "aided by staff members in touch with the constituency"; then it switches to an admonition to buy "materials" on the basis of "the present and future needs of the library." Surely my emendation is closer to what was originally intended. Or is it? Perhaps your Code means that what is good for the library is good for the constituency? Problems, problems.)

But to get back to the "materials": There is no censorship here. Publications and viewpoints of all kinds will be in your library—well, at least as far as it is "consistent with the policies of the library and with the funds available." No siree, no censorship here at all. So hold your head high, friend, and breathe in that free air.

Do you serve all the public? You had better serve them all; it is in your Code. All the public, that is, "who are entitled to use the library." If some group or class is not "entitled"—well, that lets you off the hook.

Another obligation: You are to "treat as confidential any private information" you get from library patrons. So at the next party you go to, when your host offers to "freshen" the drink you clutch—watch it, friend, watch it. Behind your host's bland and smiling face may lurk only an evil wish to get you stewed so you will blab all the sins your patrons insist on confessing to you.

And be sure you "protect library property": it is your Code. So do not sneak off with that pencil. And check your patron's pockets. But you do not really have to do that; instead, you will only "inculcate in users a sense of their responsibility" for library property's "preservation." So the poor fellow will not walk off with a pencil or a book after all. Or will he? Your Code does not say where he is to preserve the library's property. Maybe you should look to his pockets after all.

Anyway, that gets us to you and your library and your fellow librarians.

Here again your Code shakes a firm finger at your boss.

He is to delegate authority, encourage initiative, appreciate good work, tell you what your duties are, tell you the "policies and problems of the library," and help you fulfill the dreams of Horatio Alger, Jr.

Also your boss is to "provide for" your "professional development." So you are to keep up with all the new things in the library world; it is in your Code. You are to go to library association meetings and serve on committees; it is in your Code. Go ahead, do it; your boss will "provide" for it. "Provide" means get the library to foot the bill. You know, the way the library foots the bill when your boss goes to meetings and things.

Are you loyal and courteous to your fellow workers, even when they burn you? You should be; it is in your Code. And when you have a gripe you will, of course, take it to "the proper authority for the sole purpose of improvement of the library." Why, of course, you will. Even if it means the other guy gets fired. It is all in your Code.

Do you leave your job when you get a chance at a better job? Well, only if you have been where you are long enough for your boss to get back his investment in training you. And if you sign a contract, do you keep it? Will you make a "personal profit" from a "business dealing on behalf of the library"? If you have any doubts about basic library principles like these, your Code will keep you in that old straight and narrow.

Do you get a living wage for what you do? Well, your Code does not really say. But why be nitpicking all the time? Think of all the great things your Code *does* say. Service, friend, that is what counts. Service with a Smile and a capital S.

There are a lot more real helpful hints in your Code. But my list stops here. So get out your Code and read it yourself, friend.

It is really loaded.

Who Shakes The Earth Shakes Me

"But, sir," said the young man with the black beard, "what you are suggesting is the status quo."

The faculty sat around the big table and the two student representatives sat against the wall. Sally nodded in agreement with Chad. Professor Jaggsby, who was known as something of a Young Turk in NLA circles, was patient and sympathetic and low-voiced.

"No, Chad, there's something more here than just the status quo. You have had a student organization in the past, and there has been an alumni organization and there has been the faculty. What is new is that we propose an executive committee for each group with regular joint meetings of the executive committees to consider school affairs. Also we propose that there be an elected student member of every faculty committee except the committee on grievances and on appointments and promotions. The new thing is that you will have a channel of communication."

"Communicate, yes!" Sally was not as patient as Chad. "But what is communication? It's deciding that counts. What we want is a student representative with voting rights to attend all faculty meetings."

Jaggsby looked even more patient: "Actually with a vote you would have much less. In any vote taken you might be a minority of one and that would be the end of it. With the faculty proposal of a student body executive committee, the lines of communication would stay always open and your issue would still stay alive even if the faculty voted it down."

"Just as the student representative to the faculty and the student organization could keep an issue alive once it had been voted down by the faculty?" Sally's voice purred.

Jaggsby's voice raised but he spoke very slowly. "Well, really there is a difference, you know."

"What's the difference?" Sally still purred.

"Anyway," Chad cut in and saved Jaggsby for the time. "Anyway, it would not matter if now and then our representative to the faculty did propose something and vote for something which did not pass. Suppose that *did* throw him and the entire student body of 300 into a minority position. That is all beside the point. We do not ask to win everything every time. We only ask for a democratic voice in matters which affect us."

Jaggsby opened his mouth but Chad swept on. "Suppose the whole thing we ask for is a mistake. We ask only for freedom. Freedom is absolute. It is freedom to be foolish as well as freedom to be wise. We are grateful for the faculty's concern that we not ask for something foolish. But—with all due respect, sir—this concern is the paternalistic concern of the Establishment."

Miss Jonsby had little patience with Jaggsby's patience. This nonsense should come to an end. She cut in with a new attack:

"Sally, when were you elected a student representative?"

"Why—last night, Miss Jonsby; but what has that to do—"

"Last night, yes." Miss Jonsby mused. "Last night at the student rally, no doubt. How many students were there, Sally?"

"Oh, I really don't know. Quite a crowd though."

"Did any candidates oppose you two?"

"Well—no, I guess not."

"Was the vote unanimous then?"

"Yes, it sure was. Everybody shouted for us." Sally's eyes sparkled.

"Yes, I'm sure they did." Miss Jonsby's voice was a dry murmur. "Sally, how many students do you know personally?"

"Well, not a lot really. School began only last week, you know."

"Yes, I know." Miss Jonsby grew pensive. She went on slowly. "How do you propose to elect a student representative to the faculty? In the same way you were elected last night? Would you want someone you elected without really knowing him to vote for you in faculty for a full year?"

"Well, no—I suppose I wouldn't." Sally's voice almost wept. Then she brightened. "Miss Jonsby, how does the faculty suggest we go about electing members of the proposed student body executive committee?"

"Bravo, Sally! Bravo!" Quamby liked a pretty girl especially if she had ideas and spunk. He then went on.

"My learned friends, if these two young people are representative of our student body this year it looks like a mighty interesting year indeed. You will have to admit it, my dear colleagues of the Establishment—yes, Jaggsby, even you. In NLA you may dance a lively jig as a wild-eyed liberal but here you are just like the rest of us: part of the Establishment. You will have to admit it all of you: we have lost this debate."

Quamby grinned. The Dean started to speak. But Quamby was not an easy man to stop; he swept on:

"Mr. Dean, I shall vote against the proposed student representative to the faculty with full voting rights. But not for the Jaggsby-Jonsby reasons." He smiled sweetly at his colleagues. "We deserved to lose the debate if that was the best we could do. Chad was right: We offered only the paternalistic concern of the Establishment. Our argument was only a sham."

Several of the faculty tried to say something and Quamby ignored them with a smile. Chad and Sally listened in fascination.

"Our argument rests on only one fact: We are the faculty. It is our job to take bright young people like Sally and Chad and make them into better librarians than we are. This means we shall give them certain skills; but most of all it means we shall get them to think—boldly, critically, creatively. If we do this job well we shall now and then do things they will not like and things they would vote against. Even young people sometimes do not like to be made to think critically. We must always *listen* to them. But we can never do what they want simply because they want it or because they are watching us do it.

"My fair colleague" (he grinned again at Miss Jonsby) "has made much of the fact that students are here for only one year and therefore cannot have meaningful elections. But this one-year business is a lot bigger than that. When a faculty member votes for a change in policy or a change in curriculum he knows he will have to work out details of that change and he knows he will be here next year and the year after to be blamed if that change goes sour. After a student votes he leaves in a few months. But a vote is not just a vote; it is a responsibility. We are the faculty. When we vote we lay ourselves and our school on the line."

Epilogue

Once upon a time there was a young librarian who, ever since he had been knee-high to a charging desk, had dreamed of being one day a journalist. Like others before him, he traveled across the seas to the land of opportunity, and opportunity, as it is supposed to in that land, beckoned. He became indeed a journalist, with all the pages of the library Bible spread out before him at his command.

The fledgling journalist loved perhaps one American above all others, an Oriole called Mencken, and he cherished the muckrakers of earlier (pre-Agnew) days. He determined to try to bring some of this spirit to what is loosely known as the literature of librarianship. Under his command the library Bible began to take on a fiery earnestness and the smoke of many "causes" curled from its pages.

But the journalist had, also from those knee-high days, been reared on the words and irreverances of a red-headed Irishman named Shaw, despite that writer's assertion that people should not adopt him as their favorite author even if it was for their own good. While not exactly tiring of the crusades launched by the library Bible the journalist gradually began to become aware that many of the crusaders seemed deficient in one or other of the qualities he had come, through Shavian saturation, to expect of words assembled together on paper—notably wit and style and some sustained effort to make men take themselves less seriously (in short, perspective). He knew, of course, being older by then and a chauvinist to boot, that he could never hope to make women take themselves less seriously.

He began to search for such qualities in other, less biblical areas of the literature of librarianship and found, not these qualities but the language of Madison Avenue incongruously in bed with the frumpish footnote of academe. For a while he believed that the Americans had slaughtered wit and style and irreverance as they had slaughtered the Indians (and later the Vietnamese).

But crusaders, particularly English ones, do not give up easily, and our journalist pursued his quest into even the most incredibly unlikely realms, even into the literature of cataloging. In the pages of a publication with a ghastly, bifurcated, even schizophrenic title—*Library Resources and Technical Services*—he discovered at last what he was looking for. And he proposed. Surely a man who could write not just with wisdom but with wit about *cataloging* could bring his gifts to just about any topic. Come write for my library Bible, the journalist pleaded. Scintillate about the whole wide captivating world of library land. Reach out from your little 5x3 ghetto. You are too good to be left in the LRTS.

The scintillating writer about cataloging was modest and reluctant but he was wooed and seduced by the persistent journalist in the end, and for a whole year he became what the journalist called a columnist. He occupied, in solitary splendor, a page second in holiness to that temple among the library Bible's pages, the editorial page, which the journalist always kept for himself.

The columnist's year was divided into twenty-two parts (being a cataloger still at heart, he called them subdivisions). As the columns followed each other in a steady stream the journalist (and even a few of the library Bible's readers who could detect that words have a shape as well

as a meaning) began to appreciate the new savor and flavor
of wit and perspective that had entered the pages of this
muckraking malcontent in the family of the literature of
librarianship. And when the year ended, the journalist (as
even were some of the readers) was sad. How often, he
philosophized in the manner of his favorite philosopher,
Lawrence F. Berra, can you hit a home run.

Even so, the journalist had not seen at the time (for
though he was earnest he was not as perceptive as he should
have been) that what the scintillating writer had wrought
was something more than twenty-two isolated exercises in
wit and wisdom about library land. These columns were in
fact the beginning of a Grand Design. The scintillating
writer had, by God, imperceptibly, fiendishly, started his
own subtle crusade. There is some excuse for the journalist:
a crusade-within-a-crusade is even harder to detect than a
conference-within-a-conference.

Perhaps what he had done—or begun—was not even clear
immediately to the scintillating writer. He returned to the
LRTS and the land of the five-by-three, though now with
status and power, controlling its destinies just as the journalist did the library Bible's. But still, his new throne at
the LRTS was little better than a Procrustean bed, and it
was scarcely visible from some of the far-out corners of
library land. The scintillating writer began to yearn for the
wide-open spaces again. Never again could he be restricted
solely to the fifteen-square-inch dimension. Freedom of
speech, as it ever was, is heady stuff.

This time *he* proposed to the journalist. What if the
twenty-two parts (subdivisions) were to multiply and become forty-four, or more? What if the parts could be so
structured, with the fiendish ingenuity of a man who knew
classification, into a whole, and what was once a mere
column could become a volume—A BOOK? Is a book not
more biblical than the holiest of periodical publications?

Whoever heard of a librarian throwing away a book? A magazine is a now medium, but the book is the foundation stone of all media. The journalist was not modest and reluctant, and he could not withstand the passion and logic of the scintillating writer's propaganda. Besides, if finding wit and perspective in the periodical literature is like looking for that proverbial needle in the haystack (who *does* sew in a haystack?), similar qualities in the books about library land are as rare as a girl at a meeting of the Melvil Dui Chowder and Marching Association. And so this book was born.

And now that it is here it is easy to see that the pieces do indeed fit together, and do form a design, grand or otherwise, depending which mousetrap you view it from. Our scintillating writer's message is whispered with a smile but its penetration is more deadly and insistent than the stridency of the journalist and his cohorts of crusaders. No lofty aims, the writer says he has. These little tales "do not pretend to be the truth, the whole truth, and nothing but." And yet . . . and yet . . . beneath the pleasant fancies there is the uncomfortable stench of an overriding truth. It is perhaps not, as another writer has told us, that truth is stranger than fiction. What this writer tells us, page after light-tripping page, is that truth (or the truth(s) we promulgate about ourselves and our profession) *is* fiction.

You were, dear librarians, better off, safer, with us simple muckrakers and journalists.

Eric Moon
June 1970.